THE ANALOGUE
APPROACH
TO DIGITAL RECORDING
AND MIXING

Fran Ashcroft

THE ANALOGUE APPROACH TO DIGITAL RECORDING AND MIXING

THE CROWOOD PRESS

First published in 2023 by
The Crowood Press Ltd
Ramsbury, Marlborough
Wiltshire SN8 2HR

enquiries@crowood.com

www.crowood.com

British Library Cataloguing-in-Publication Data
A catalogue record for this book is available from the British Library.

ISBN 978 0 7198 4176 7

Acknowledgements
Photographs by David James Wood & James Power at Material Studios,
147–161 Richmond Row, Liverpool L3 3BU. https://www.materialstudios.co

Additional expertise on how to plug things in and that, thanks to Marc Joy at
ferndaleproductions.co.uk

And Audacity's free, open-source recording and mixing software: www.audacityteam.org

Typeset by Jean Cussons Typesetting, Diss, Norfolk
Cover design by Sergey Tsvetkov
Printed and bound in India by Parksons Graphics

CONTENTS

INTRODUCTION

ANYONE FOR ANALOGUE?

'Everything that is easy on analogue is difficult on digital; everything that is difficult on digital is easy on analogue' – 'old Chinese proverb'

There are a lot of myths about recording and some seriously misguided ideas of how you're supposed to go about it. Recording is simple. You put a microphone in front of the sound you want and press record. That's it. There is nothing you *have* to do, no rule book that says you must EQ and compress or manipulate it afterwards. It's entirely up to you.

Digital recording presents a world of endless options, where all decisions can be postponed indefinitely. 'Make your mind up later' is a strong selling point, but the truth is, digital is not particularly user-friendly. Analogue represents the opposite; its limitations force you to make fast, often intuitive decisions that cut out the middleman and just finish the record. By adopting some analogue thinking and adapting its techniques in the digital realm, you can revolutionise your recordings – not just in the way they sound, but in the way they feel. This takes a completely different mindset than 'plug it in and fix it later'.

Digital systems were not designed by recording engineers and some of the fundamental aspects have been badly thought out. For example, changing a volume level by selecting the sound and using a 'pencil' tool to draw it with a mouse is a hopeless idea. When digital recording encourages you to solve problems by using more complex technology, it's good for them, of course – you have to buy more stuff. Upgrade now, or your system won't work any more.

Recorded sounds are not independent of each other; how they work with their companions, their behaviour and the unique interplay between them is a keystone of recording. Manipulating a sound in isolation doesn't work well if you can't hear it in context quickly and easily and can send you into a tailspin of knob twiddling and tweaking in no time. The better you can compare sounds in context, the more effective the results will be. Unfortunately, digital is lacking in this respect, when you can't click on two things at once with a computer mouse, or turn two knobs at the same time. It's apt to be time-consuming if the most necessary functions are often impractical.

On average, you might spend six hours a day on a mix session. You start making poor choices after that. And the length of time things take is important – because it's all creative time. In real terms, at least half the work will be preparatory, such as fixing levels, fine-tuning sounds and so on. Balancing the mix is the big deal – and there's a short performance curve on that. Believe me, I hit a peak at about forty-five minutes in. You can feel it. Pass that peak and you're in for a long haul to get back. Which is why it's not out of the ordinary to take a week or longer to mix a track digitally that would have taken a maximum of a day and a half on analogue.

It is a challenge not to be a perfectionist when recording digitally. It's unsympathetic to errors and the workflow can be onerous; mixing forty tracks of sound rather than a mere sixteen takes a lot longer and you simply can't connect with it in the same way. But don't for a moment think that analogue recording is all about the type of equipment you use. It's mostly about how you use the technology you've got.

In their heyday, recording studios were unique spaces, each with their own sonic signatures. Abbey Road and Trident were both as good as you could get – but sounded quite different from each other. So, at the outset, the question of 'What studio should we use?' was a significant choice. It's not like that anymore. Everywhere sounds the same because the technology is more or less identical. It's a sad paradox – now that there are no limits to the number of tracks and effects you can use, it is a whole universe

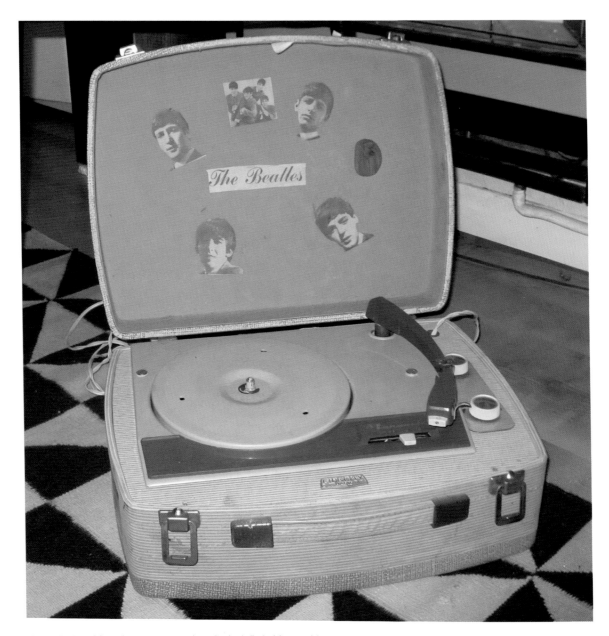

'Record player' found at a recent archaeological dig in Merseyside.

of possibilities. Yet recording has become more homogenised than it has ever been. Maybe there are so many choices, we all just opt out and go to the hamburger joint.

It is your approach to the process that matters. Key decisions are made early on in analogue recording, unlike digital where the software encourages you to postpone them. If it's more convenient to open up a new track and save three alternates than do a punch-in and record over an error, you end up fixing all kinds of performance shortcomings when you mix, which will end up taking so long that you lose any sense of spontaneity you might have had when you began.

Getting the most out of analogue recording did need preparation and forethought. You had to figure out in advance what you wanted on the front end, because there were not many fixes possible after the fact; you had to get it right at the time. Quite simply, if you didn't have a pretty good idea of what the finished recording would turn out like before you started, you would be heading for trouble. There was no safety net and I believe that element of risk added more energy and focus to the proceedings. The lack of 'feel' attributed to digital is as much to do with that as the sound itself.

THAT ANALOGUE SOUND

What do you think of as the sound of analogue recording? Is it a vinyl record, tape compression, the preamps and valves, the microphones, or what? Do you mean the sound of 1950s recording? 1960s? 1970s? They are all very different from each other.

What I can tell you is that it is definitely *not* about adding another piece of equipment to your arsenal to use like a plug-in. It's an integrated, start-to-finish process; a way of working. How you think about and prepare for your recordings and all the decisions you make along the way are more important than any equipment you use. That approach can be adapted to a digital environment. You don't

need a big rack full of vintage compressors or an expensive mixing desk. You don't need a tape recorder (nice as they may be, though you would be lucky to find one in decent working order). Your choice of gear or your budget has no bearing on the way you choose to work – that costs nothing.

There is no such thing as a 'good' sound. Or a 'bad' one, either. That's rather like saying there are good and bad colours. I'd stretch the point to say there's no such thing as good or bad equipment. It's a matter of taste, how you use it and the choices you make. Incorporating analogue methods and techniques will improve your recording skills across the board, no matter what kind of record it is, or the equipment you happen to have.

It is the way of thinking that is the biggest divide between analogue and digital. Many of the myths that surround recording today are a consequence of technological progress in the past; and all are as untrue now as they were then. You do *not* have to EQ everything by default, or isolate musicians in booths, or stick a mic on every component of a drum kit. Really.

If I were to pose the question: 'Did we make good records before parametric EQ or multiband compression was invented?', you would reply, 'Yes, of course we did.'

Then I might say, 'Well, you don't really need parametric EQ or multiband compression, do you?'

But *of course* you can make sounds on digital that are just as effective as analogue, though it is still a different animal. There's a human element to analogue recordings that everyone can relate to, a certain enchantment in a vinyl disc spinning on a record player. I'm not surprised that records are popular again, and not just because of nostalgia. The resurgence of vinyl has largely been fuelled by a young, digital generation, tired of throwaway corporate pop. Vinyl still has its own unique, indefinable magic – and some of it might just rub off on you, as you take it out of the sleeve, mightn't it? CDs and downloads could never hope to compete with that.

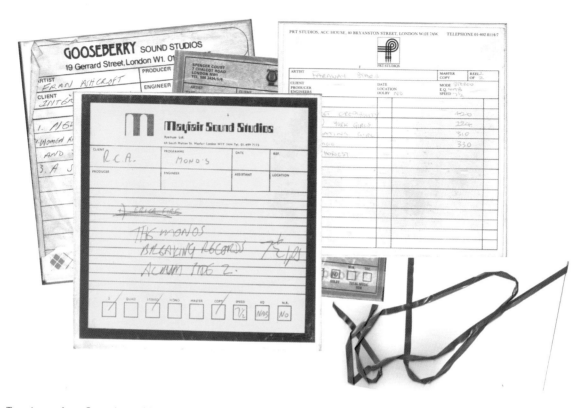

Tape boxes from Gooseberry, Mayfair, Utopia and Pye studios.

The recording industry is driven by profit and will take any opportunity to sell a new but not necessarily improved version of a product that is fundamentally the same. What may be fashionable is not always better. Were CDs really superior to vinyl? Did you get rid of your record collection, only to replace it with the 'remastered vinyl' versions ten years later?

Despite everything, analogue is enduring, maybe because it is remarkably good at capturing our feelings and memories. It carries them well. It is a process that feels *in the moment* and *captures* that moment. Digital doesn't really do that, does it? By comparison, it feels impermanent and disposable. No matter what technical wizardry digital can conjure up, analogue is still the yardstick against which results are measured. All that is quick and easy on analogue may well be longwinded and monotonous on digital, but on the plus side, all

the things that were impossible on analogue are at your digital fingertips.

It is only very recently that recording has become available to everyone. This is a privilege. In the not too distant past, you needed very deep pockets, or to be contracted to a large corporation. You could only record when you were allowed to and in the way you were told. Thankfully, this is no longer the case and you are completely free to do whatever you want, with a huge array of tools at your disposal.

You may have a home studio or a professional set-up. Either way, you will probably know some of what follows. You might disagree with it, but I encourage you to keep an open mind. Recording need not be complicated, even if everything that surrounds it seems to be. It certainly used to be simpler and there's no reason it can't be more straightforward now. Choosing to take an analogue approach to digital recording will change the way you work. It is fastest and easiest if you have an analogue mixer integrated into your system, but this is certainly not a requirement. Mixing on a control surface with faders will take a little longer, and it may be more demanding if you're completely 'in the box', but preparation and recording is the same, regardless.

The first time you embark on recording and mixing with these analogue techniques will be quite different to the way you've done things in the past. It might appear unfamiliar and unorthodox as you read through the instructions the first time. Consider it a reset of how you think about the entire process. We're starting at square one, from the room you record in, the format you're working with, right through to recording, mixing and mastering your finished recordings.

1

YOUR STUDIO

Forget all your preconceptions about recording studios and their design. Digital technology has changed the landscape. Modern studios fall into two categories – traditional rooms to record groups of musicians in, and single, control-room spaces with little or no separate recording area.

ACOUSTICS

Find a room that music sounds good in. It's difficult to make a bad-sounding room sound good. It is not true that you *must* have acoustic treatments in your room; however, you do need a pleasant-sounding room and monitors that tell you the truth. If it's a poor room, try to find another.

Sound travels through the air and bounces around all the objects in its path. The reflections can be pleasing or horrid, and every room will have its weaknesses. The imperfections are magnified in relation to the volume at which you listen. The simplest way to check where sonic problems lie within any room is to play some familiar music through your monitors, starting at a low volume, then gradually increasing it. Past a certain point, the sound will become uneven, harsh or muddy. Back off the level to the point where the sound is most detailed and defined, mark the master volume on your recorder or amp, and don't monitor anything above that level.

That's fine as long as you're happy to work at whatever that volume happens to be. Otherwise, your room will need acoustic treatment of some kind. Some very simple things can help in a domestic environment: if your room is harsh, or

too 'live', it may need nothing more than a carpet on the floor and long curtains for the windows or walls to soften it. Try that first. To isolate external noise and reduce sound escaping from the studio, weatherstrip the door tightly and use a double layer of rubber underlay beneath the carpet (the heavy, dense kind, not foam rubber). This works well to isolate lower frequencies travelling through joists into adjacent rooms. Rubber underlay is also handy placed under monitors if they are not free-standing and also to isolate computer noise.

Recording in a modest room does not mean you can't get a good result, if you think it through well. For example, Tamla Motown's studio was a 4 × 5m (13 × 16.5ft) room with all the musicians crammed in, recorded live, including vocals – without any isolation booths, baffles or headphones. Is that cool, or what? Get to know your room. Think of installing soundproofing, bass traps and so on only as a last resort and, if you do, try movable options first. Sticking egg boxes all over the walls will not do you any good. I've done a lot of records in my mastering studio, certainly in the region of 3,000 tracks. It's an unexceptional, 3 × 2.5m (10 × 8ft) room, with no acoustic treatment at all – other than a carpet and purple psychedelic curtains.

I am hesitant to recommend soundproofing and acoustic treatments, as they don't always have the desired result. The owner of one of London's most expensive studios spent a quarter of a million building a mix room that turned out to be hopelessly inaccurate and he had to rip it out and start all over again within two weeks of opening. So, keep acoustic treatments as simple as possible –

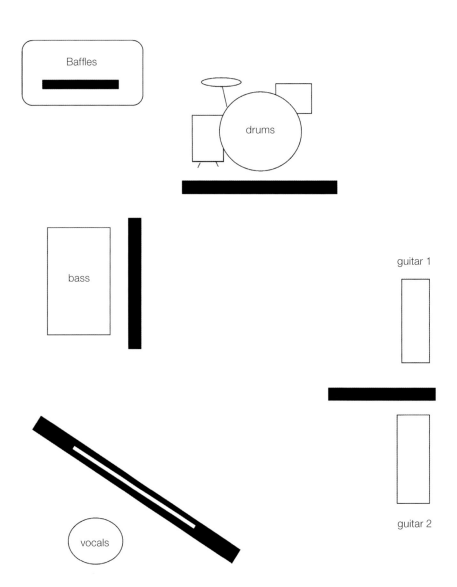

and preferably portable. Free-standing baffles or movable acoustic panels will provide a much more flexible environment.

RECORDING SPACES

You may have a room large enough to accommodate several musicians, or have a separate room for them. Assuming there's no significant spillage and noise escaping to warrant the neighbours complaining to the council, and if it sounds okay to you, leave it alone. But you may not just have a neighbour problem – the louder the noise level, the more reflections there are in the room, which can be very unpleasant to hear if you happen to be in there at the time. In that event, if you can't turn it down a bit, I'm afraid you're probably in for the full 'studio' treatment – 2 × 4 battens attached to every wall and with the ceiling stuffed with as much sound-insulation material as can be crammed in, before plasterboarding over the lot. I have been in studios that did not bother with the plasterboard and just left the fibreglass insulation to disperse gradually around the room. Don't try that.

Once your recording space is complete, you will want to put musicians inside it. For a regular, amplified band line-up, you will probably need some baffles to contain the loudest instruments from spilling too much into the others. Some bleed is fine, but not if the bass is leaking all over the drums and vocals. You can buy ready-made baffles, or make your own. They are just narrow boxes in various sizes with sound insulation in them, or office-like screens, sometimes with a window in, useful if you plan on recording live vocals. Of course, you can just pile up empty guitar cases with your coats on top in an emergency.

MONITORING

The monitoring system is the most important component of your studio. If your speakers are not telling the truth, every decision you make will be compromised. I was once asked, why do some engineers like to have monitors on their side and others prefer them upright? This is not something I'd consciously thought about before, but it's very simple – turn them on their side and there's more

Yamaha, large Dynatron and small Tannoy monitors.

room to put your cups on the top. No, not really. It's all down to how we perceive sound. We're all individual in what we like to hear when we work – loud or quiet, bass-heavy, bass-light, near or far – a lot of factors are involved. I'm generally in favour of upright, large, three-way speakers.

Accurate monitoring can be alarmingly expensive and 'home studio' speakers are priced to kill. It's important to note that modern monitors tend to be boosted in the lows, with a lift in the high end. All the action is *really* in the mids, but it's hard to find small monitors that represent this well.

It's common now for active, near-field speakers to be the main monitors in a studio, yet they can be wildly inaccurate and inconsistent. The designs are still largely based on the original near-field monitors, Yamaha NS10s. Limited as they are – with a rather crushed mid-range to say the least – so many studios bought them, they became the de facto standard that others have been measured against ever since.

It's been forgotten that NS10s were never intended to be accurate in the first place; they were supposed to be merely a representation of what a mix would sound like on the radio, a quick, second point of reference. And, with a bit of guesswork, they did a reasonably good job. Typically, you would monitor through the big speakers during recording, then flip back and forth between the main monitors and the NS10s when you mixed. Over time, NS10s became the monitoring favourite, which is bizarre but fits with my as yet unproven theory that as technology 'improves' the fidelity (or shall we say 'attractiveness') of sound, it deteriorates by the same amount. This is due to manufacturers of domestic audio equipment selling playback systems and formats that are cheaper for them to produce, such as MP3 players or earbuds, which sound so naff that it doesn't make much difference if you file-compress a mix to destruction.

Testing Your Monitoring System for Accuracy

Set up your amplifier and speakers with the amplifier tone controls at 0 (no *loudness* or *extra bass/*

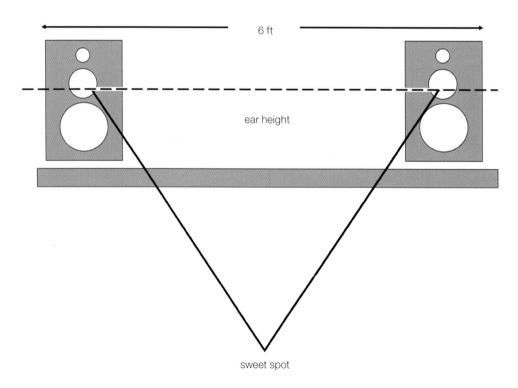

6 ft

ear height

sweet spot

Diagram showing monitor placement.

sub bass please). Position the speakers 2m (6.5ft) apart, with the mid-range cones at ear height. Choose several pieces of music of different styles and eras that you understand well. As you listen, turn up the volume to a comfortable level – not too loud – where the sonics are best represented, moving your listening position and distance to find the 'sweet spot' where the stereo image is most cohesive and spatial. Sometimes angling the speakers slightly inwards will enhance this. Can you hear any low-end bulge or high harshness in this spot? If so, turn down the volume and see if it disappears. Still there? Check that the bass is not resonating through another surface, by lifting the speakers from the shelf they are on, or moving them away from the wall. Also cross-check your ear position in relation to the speakers by tilting your head forward and back, and up and down a few inches.

If your room is a small one which doesn't allow much depth between you and the monitors, bring the speakers in from 2m (6.5ft) to as little as 1.25m (4ft) apart, angled slightly towards your ears. This creates a modified sweet spot and though it reduces stereo imaging, it isn't a liability. Monitoring at close quarters means listening at lower volume levels, otherwise you'll have ear burnout in no time.

Your ears quickly become accustomed to the sound of your monitors, so it's vital to make some test recordings and check for accuracy in several different environments on various sound systems, from audiophile to laptop speakers. This allows you to set reference points and adjust accordingly for sonic imperfections. When cross-referencing outside your studio, listen carefully for particular frequency areas that seem dominant or lumpy, or if the perceived balance of your mixes is affected on all of the reference systems. Listen for 'holes' in the sound and inconsistencies that occur, making notes on your first impressions. The sound systems that you cross-reference with, and the spaces they are in, will each have their own characteristics and none will be completely true; but your aim is to build up a picture of anything that sounds inaccurate in all of the alternate environments.

When you have identified problem areas, try some minor tone control adjustments before resorting to soundproofing or acoustic treatments. Your monitors may have some limited EQ settings on the back, so try that first. Otherwise, you can optimise the tone settings on your power amp. Don't overanalyse. If your ears are tired, nothing will make sense. Swift, instinctive decisions with fresh ears yield the best results, which may mean short listening sessions spread over a number of days, or even weeks. It takes time and patience, but you won't regret it.

Ultimately, you can't expect any room to be completely accurate, so you have to go with what sounds most representative OUTSIDE of your studio. Over time, you'll get to know the quirks of your monitors very well and how to compensate for imperfections. It's also handy to have a second pair of speakers for cross-referencing – typically cheap and nasty ones. Always check your work in other rooms, on computer speakers, a terrible modern bookshelf stereo (for muddiness) and a decent hi-fi system (if you can find one).

Should you come to the conclusion that your monitors are too inaccurate, you will have to replace them. Beware the hype – and always check the specs thoroughly. You want something with the flattest, most even response, with detailed mid range and not overly flattering. If you've never tried a large three-way speaker system, give it a go; their character is very different to active monitors. But whatever you decide on, listen and listen again; compare your choices carefully before shelling out your cash!

EQUIPMENT

I must emphasise that you don't have to buy anything to incorporate analogue methods into your recordings. How you approach and adapt the *process* is the more important thing. There is nothing you really need to spend, other than your time – okay, maybe you need a microphone or two, or perhaps another set of speakers. Software is freely available; outboard gear, analogue mixers, expensive preamps or glowing blue valves are not required. If you do want to invest in gear, get the absolute minimum and choose wisely. Yet another compressor or reverb won't solve problems you encounter and too much gear – whether plug-ins or outboard – can only open a Pandora's Box of options, and hinders as much as it helps. Resist the temptation. If you do happen to add new software or programs, get them from a reliable source. There are lots of scammers and hackers out there. Going to the manufacturer or developer's website is generally the best course of action.

RECORDERS

For hardcore analogophiles, there are still tape recorders knocking around, but they're all in the autumn of their lives. It's very difficult finding one in decent working order, regardless of price. Expect it to need servicing, at the very least. Spare parts are scarce, techs are thin on the ground and even if you're lucky enough to come across a tape recorder that works properly, unused tape is expensive. And you still end up having to transfer your recordings into a digital format for people to listen to them. A reel to reel might just be impractical to use; it may sound great – *except for the hiss*. Currently, I have two reel to reels and roughly eight cassette decks; just two are usable. The other six make handy fuzzboxes.

For the most part, digital audio workstations (DAWs) have superseded hard disc recorders, portastudios and the like. They are king, for the moment, being cheap – even free – and readily available to all. While computer-based systems are excellent for editing, or cutting and pasting samples and loops, they are not quite so intuitive if your aim is to record live musicians in real time, or to work in an analogue style. Digital formats like Pro Tools have steep learning curves and simple, important things can be frustratingly slow. There are some workarounds to make life easier, but basically, what we'd really like around here is a computer program that operates with the ease of a tape recorder.

That being said, Pro Tools and Logic (or the most recent versions of them) now include a 'quick punch' facility that allows the user to record and punch in on the fly, *on the same track*! Which I applaud, although making quick level changes within that track is still incomprehensible to me. The free program Audacity also has a similar, if clunkier, 'punch and roll' feature, with level edits relatively easy to manage. Other major platforms have a range of more baffling solutions – so how simple or frustrating the process is will depend entirely on what you are using.

Functionality is important, but only insofar as it affects the timeliness of the process as a whole. If you can maintain a steady workflow with momentum, it won't matter if a mix took half an hour or a week. Understand your own performance habits; how long your concentration span is and plan around that. You might feel in the zone for twenty minutes or two hours, so work to your strengths and allow for your shortcomings.

INTERFACES

Digital recording interfaces can be as basic as a little box with a line and mic input that you plug into your computer's sound card, or in groups of four, eight or more channels, all of which you can record on at the same time, with the software of your choice. Basically, the little box talks to your computer and the computer says okay then. Or you can go the whole hog and get an interface with a control surface built in, which you can sort of operate with faders. I say 'sort of', as often there are only four small faders, so you have to shuttle back and forth from fader bank to fader bank all the time with the more tracks you use. This little box asks the computer if it's okay for it to remember fader moves and twiddled knobs on your mixes as well, which is very accommodating of it.

If you're using an interface already, you'll be familiar with this to some extent. When you're on the cusp of buying one, make sure that it has the correct system requirements for your computer.

Ribbon microphone.

Interfaces commonly come bundled with record-ing software, which you may want to use, or not. If you're already using recording software you like, it's probably best to keep the one you're accus-tomed to, in the interests of saving time, hard disc space and, quite possibly, money. So in this case say 'nyet' when it asks if you want to install the latest subscription-based version of '_____' (*insert your least favourite software manufactur-er's name here*). Read the fine print, always.

PLUG-INS

Plug-ins are the DAW's companion. How many lifetimes would it take to audition all of them currently circulating the planet? I think we'd be underwater first. Your recording platform will already be loaded to the gills with them. Most are useless and sound awful. Just pick a small hand-

Beyer M201
microphone.

Sennheiser 441
microphone.

Neumann
microphone.

ful and choose carefully. All you really need are one or two compressors, a limiter, an EQ, reverb and delay. The challenge is finding the ones that suit you – so you'll need to listen to more than a few before deciding on your favourites. Bear in mind that they have to work with each other, so it's helpful if your choices share tonally similar, complementary signatures. The other benefit to only using a handful of plug-ins is that you'll get to know them well enough to customise settings precisely for your needs.

Menu presets are a handy starting point, but nothing more. Only consider plug-ins that are intuitive to operate, with few bells and whistles and that have warmth, detail and clarity. They shouldn't do anything other than enhance the sounds you run through them. My supposedly 'high-end' software has at least fifty-plus effects in it; I only use three of them regularly and just two additional ones, both of which were free downloads. I use one consistently, the other on occasion.

Sennhesier 421
microphone.

Shure 57
microphone.

Microphones

Remember this – *the performance is always more important than the microphone*. Microphones are everywhere, aren't they? Some are cheap and nasty, some cheap and not nasty at all, others are overpriced rubbish, while some are very expensive and very good. The choice is vast, so how do you make a decision on which are best for you? It's a bit of a hype minefield.

Mostly, people end up buying what they can afford, then gradually expand and replace their mics as funds allow, finding microphones most suited to their needs by trial and error. You'll buy more than you really want to and make one or two mistakes along the way – who needs a set of clip-on mics for drums, really? Two or three dynamics and a couple of condensers will do the job to begin with. And I should note that any microphone can be used in all sorts of applications. You don't necessarily need a special one for the kick drum, or even a vocal. Be creative – you can work with whatever you happen to have.

Manufacturers know that gearheads like to rhapsodise about microphones; I lost count a long time ago of the number of clones to claim they're *just like* a Neumann U47. Take microphone reviews with a large pinch of salt. Many manufacturers advertise in 'pay to play' publications and forums, and reviewers generally get to keep the products they endorse. So there might be some bias involved, d'yer think?

If you're familiar with how microphones behave, it will save a lot of bother, so be sure to familiarise yourself with the specs. The pick-up patterns, frequency range, lift and roll off – that is, how a mic is 'tuned' by the manufacturer – tell you a lot. Study the frequency graph (even if they are sometimes fanciful) and don't be fooled by appearance. I once bought a little microphone on the strength of it looking like a bug with two antennae. It didn't sound great, even though it did say 'Realistic' on the box!

The most common types of microphones are dynamic and condenser.

Dynamic microphones are versatile, durable workhorses, able to withstand high volume levels, equally at home on a guitar or a snare drum. The Shure SM57 is the quintessential directional dynamic mic, universal on stage and in the studio. It will work on anything, take a thrashing, and always deliver a half decent sound. Though it lacks a bit of a detail, the mid-range and proximity effect of this mic can help out an otherwise thin signal, which is probably one reason why it's so popular for close micing of electric guitars. Shure's SM58 is principally the same thing in a different casing, with a slightly more open characteristic.

Condenser microphones are somewhat more delicate and refined, with more depth and detail, and are well suited to natural sounds. Although there are variations, dynamics are usually directional, whereas condensers favour a wider, cardioid, pick-up pattern. They come in all shapes, sizes and prices, from small electret condensers powered by a battery, to large 5cm (2in) diaphragm models in custom suspension mounts. Most require phantom power from a mixing desk, a preamp, or their own power supply. Some condensers include pad and roll-off switches; the pad switch cuts the input level to prevent damage to the mic at high volumes, while roll-off cuts low frequencies. More sophisticated models have switchable pick-up patterns too, from cardioid to figure of eight – which effectively is a cardioid pattern on each side of the microphone.

Condensers can cost a lot of money, but while plenty of them are overpriced, it is still possible to buy a pair for as little as £50. If you happen to have a crushingly expensive Neumann U47, it will take care of anything you want to throw at it. But for those of us with a less lavish lifestyle, a pair of small- or medium-capsule condensers and two or three modest dynamic mics will be fine.

Other types of microphones include ribbon microphones – which have a warm, rich sound, but low output level – omnidirectional, hypercardioid, stereo, levalier mics, underwater mics. You name it, there's probably a mic for it, but aside from perhaps deep-sea exploration, I'm sure you'll get by quite well with what you already have.

HEADPHONES

You should have a pair of accurate headphones for judging mic positioning, with plenty of padding around the earpieces to keep out extraneous noise. They'll also be handy for editing, when you need to zoom in and concentrate on the exact places to cut and paste edits, but don't make mixing decisions with them. Things tend to sound different than they really are when pumping directly into your ears.

CABLES

Balanced XLR or TRS ¼in, or unbalanced ¼in, $1/_8$in minijacks and RCA Phono cables? It doesn't matter, unless you intend to run a lot of long ones. In which case, use Balanced XLRs on everything. They are more resistant to ground loop hum and are sturdier, but by no means a requirement, especially in a small studio or home environment where you don't use many and distances are short. I don't even have a problem using microphones that have attached, short cables with $1/_8$in connectors and the like. An adaptor works fine if you need a longer reach. Keep a few spares of all the kinds of cables you use the most; none last forever and the shops will inevitably have closed five minutes before your last ¼in jack in the patch bay packs up.

OUTBOARD GEAR

When using a DAW, you won't really need any outboard gear, as there is a wealth of compression, EQ, delay and lots more already in the software. The sonics are often better than low-priced outboard equipment, if less intuitive to operate. But some of you may wish to go the whole analogue hog and pig out on outboard gear. The expense usually limits how far you go. There are some exceptions, but, as a rule, good outboard isn't cheap. If you use plug-ins alongside physical outboard, be careful – the digital-effects process-

ing can easily drain the character from your physical gear.

If you're using an analogue mixing desk, some outboard gear might be necessary or preferable. A decent compressor or two, a reverb unit and a delay are handy, but a rack crammed full of exciters, EQs, chorus, noise gates and whatnot is a big waste of time. It's much better to spend your cash on fewer, better items that will be used daily. Outboard can be just as addictive as plug-ins for some people. I've known studios that have bought so much of the stuff, they could never, ever recoup the cost, even if they ran sessions twenty-four hours a day non-stop for a year. It's the eternal quest for the perfect compressor, the incredible preamp, that magic piece of kit that makes everything sound wonderful – a real Don Quixote job.

I own a Nullatron, a little black box with red and green lights that flash on and off as it operates. I don't know what it is, or what it does, and neither does anyone else who's heard it. We just agree that it does do *something*.

CLASSIC GEAR

There are software and hardware clones of 'classic' equipment appearing on a regular basis, everything from preamps to EQs to tape simulators. No matter how clever software designers are at replicating the exact specifications of the originals, there is one big omission; the software doesn't have valves, capacitors, transformers, hand-wired circuits and so on, all of which contributed to the sound of the equipment. It's very difficult writing algorithms for those sorts of things.

'Classic' analogue equipment was always very, very expensive – the province of the few. And believe me, there was always plenty of analogue gear that wasn't that great, so don't get all dewy-eyed about the good old days. To date, I have not come across a digital EQ that I like, but I could say that about a lot of analogue consoles too.

If you have been fortunate enough to use a Neve EQ, GML, or a Focusrite Red, you will immediately have noticed that the character of the sound is

A Nullatron. What does it do? We haven't a clue!

enhanced simply by running a signal through it. That's what you're paying for. It's idiot-proof gear, really. Turn the knobs whatever way you like; the sound will still be better: very popular with A&R men who try their hands at producing. Everyone would love a roomful of that kind of stuff, but we are mere mortals and use what we have. Which is in no way a bad thing; you learn how to get a result out of what is available. It sets you free when you realise that *none of this is about the gear*. Your skill, vision, talent – whatever you want to call it – is not dependent on that.

INTEGRATING AN ANALOGUE MIXER WITH YOUR DAW

To integrate an analogue console for mixing with a DAW, you need to have an audio interface with the same number of inputs as your mixer, or add additional boxfuls of A/D converters for the total number of tracks you wish to run. Typically, they come in racks of eight. The prices are not always unreasonable, but will stack up in proportion to the total number you need. That enables you to route each mixer channel to its own track in the DAW and to use the mixer's faders without automation. You should still be able to use effects and plug-ins from your DAW and/or run outboard gear

through the analogue mixer. Of course, you do have to consider the practicalities. You will need a mixer that doesn't adversely colour the signal and you must have a computer powerful enough to run all those tracks at once, without latency or other problems, so I would advise a consultation with your local tech wizard before taking the plunge.

An analogue mixer integrated to your interface allows you to get closer to the customary techniques of analogue mixing, as you can operate the faders freely and more intuitively. It's the ability to balance the tracks as you mix, in real time – that's the draw. If you're not used to it, then live-performance mixing on an analogue mixer won't be easy at first. But it's definitely a buzz to mix that way; you're physically attached to the mix and the fader choreography is akin to playing an instrument. And it is very fast to mix, by comparison.

But analogue mixers don't change the way you record the tracks. You set levels and press record, pause and stop in exactly the same manner, whether a mixer is added or not; the only difference will be the sound of the mixer and any outboard equipment running with it. A mixer in itself doesn't give you an 'analogue' sound – their characteristics vary. Some are clean (*too clean* in some ways), others might be somewhat muddy,

Got any spare A/D converters, anyone?

or overly crisp, while others might enhance the sound – generally the very expensive ones. Just how expensive increases with the number of tracks you intend to use.

Do you want four, eight, sixteen, twenty-four or more tracks? Only you can say, but I'd probably guess you'd be aiming for sixteen plus; do the maths and figure out what your budget will stand. If you want to go completely old-school analogue, you might opt for a more affordable four or eight tracks. But bear in mind that your mixes have to be built in a series of bounces if you exceed that

Bounced Mixes

When recording technology only offered two, four, eight – or any number of tracks – the same limits applied. If you needed more, you had to bounce some of them together to make extra room on the tape. And those bounced tracks could not be changed at a later point.

When you bounce tracks, you must be aware of how the balance of those instruments will behave in the context of the final mix, along with any cues they have – guitar solos and such – as well as the amount and type of effects applied to them. This is so that once the remaining components are added – vocals or other overdubs – the relationship between instruments and vocals will be balanced correctly and the record will be as you intended. That sounds easier than it actually is, especially when you multiply the number of bounces and fader choreography sometimes needed to achieve it.

Let's assume that you have just four faders on an analogue mixer to work with, interfaced with your computer, and you've recorded a total of sixteen tracks to be mixed. Load them up and make a balance between the first four tracks on the mixer, with any effects or cues they may have. You can listen to this in context with the other twelve if you wish, though it can be more interesting not to.

number. I personally like working on 4-track, but if you're accustomed to using a lot more, it would be a bit of a learning curve to master.

HOW MANY TRACKS IS ENOUGH?

One of the most enduring myths and selling points in recording has been the endless quest for more and more tracks, which grew out of a real need to overdub efficiently in the 1960s. Prior to 4-track, overdubs could only be made by bouncing sounds from one tape machine to another – sound on sound – with a generation of fidelity lost each time.

Even though 4-track offered more flexibility in mixing, complex recordings still entailed bouncing tracks, which needed imagination and very effective arrangements to work well. When you're printing reverbs, EQs and balances to an irreversible submix bounce, you have to leave room for everything else that will be added later to the final mix picture. You can't postpone decisions until mixing, or recall and fix anything, so it means using your ears and brain to the max. Get it wrong and you have to start all over again.

The introduction of 8-track brought more scope for alternate vocal takes, solos and so on, which hadn't been possible before (some people wondered what they would do with all those extra tracks!). In turn, 16- and 24-track opened the door on using a separate track for every instrument – and, in more recent times, every component of every instrument with multiple microphones, plus every effect on each component on every track. In stereo.

There might now be limitless tracks available, but you should give serious thought as to how many are actually practical. It is senseless to record forty tracks of vocals and comp them when you mix. There's no question that a single track with a real, emotive vocal will always be more effective. Apply that thinking to all aspects of a recording and the amount of tracks anyone could ever need shrinks dramatically. As a bonus, fewer tracks make for recordings with more realism and feel, as well as more manageable, dynamic mixes.

The notion that somehow a studio must be better if it has more tracks is a persistent one, but complete nonsense. I defy anyone to justify 1,982 tracks of anything. If you're using more than sixteen to twenty-four tracks, you just haven't thought it through. You've overmiked the drums, recorded too many instruments in stereo, layered up unnecessary parts, or kept too many alterna-

When you have done that, mute the other twelve tracks and bounce down the first four as a stereo mix. Next, mute or remove the first four tracks, insert your bounced mix of tracks one to four and unmute tracks five to eight. Monitor your bounced mix and balance tracks five to eight into a new bounced mix, so that you have two bounced mixes: tracks one to four and five to eight.

Repeat the process on the next two groups of four tracks and you will have four stereo mixes:

- bounce one: tracks one to four
- bounce two: tracks five to eight
- bounce three: tracks nine to twelve
- bounce four: tracks thirteen to sixteen.

You balance and bounce these together into your final mix – and that, ladies and gentlemen, is how you can make a 16-track, old-school analogue mix, with only four channels available.

ARTIST				DATE		TIMES	
	TRACK	**MIC**	**LINE**	**STUDIO LAYOUT**			**SCHEDULE**
1							
2							
3							
4							
5							
6							
7							
8							
9							
10							
13							
14							
15							
16							
17							
18							
19							
20				**OTHER REQUIREMENTS**			
21							
22							
23							
24							

Typical 24-track track sheet.

tive takes – all of which make for overworked, overprocessed, unimaginative mixes. Don't let a digital format encourage you to use tracks simply because they are available or convenient, or you will end up with eighty-four channels of rubbish that you'll be trying to create a performance out of later on. Ask yourself what you can take out, not what you can add. It focuses your attention on developing the parts and the relationships between them in the most effective way.

A restricted number of tracks is not suitable for everything or everyone, but an economical approach and some planning will never do any harm.

LATENCY

A related issue with digital recording is latency, where tracks won't synchronise any more. It's most commonly caused by running too many tracks – and/or effects – at the same time; your computer can't perform the number of tasks you are asking it to do quickly enough. The solution is usually either to use fewer tracks/fx, or add more RAM memory. Some recording platforms are prone to this (that is, the program itself can't cope) and that requires a software fix you will be delighted to spend hours Googling.

A good excuse for a B side.

GAIN STRUCTURE

Gain structure is nothing more than checking that the volume levels in your system and the applications you use are set correctly. You can read a lot of engineer-speak waffle on the subject, quoting optimal dB figures and LUFS standards, which make it sound like an intimidating thing. It isn't. Just take a look at your input and output volume levels for playback and recording on your computer/DAW, plus the plug-ins you use, then make sure that the signals are strong enough without clipping or distortion. Often the factory defaults are fine, but occasionally they're not automatically set up.

In the very early days of Pro Tools (8-track!), I was on a session in Denmark and there was an awful digital hiss (yes, it does exist) on everything. It turned out that there were multiple mixer settings within the software that had never been set up when it was installed. Once I'd been through them and corrected that, everything was fine. But I still don't understand why Pro Tools needed all those little 'mixers' in the first place.

FIDELITY

The biggest single difference between analogue and digital resolution was this; with digital, the hiss and noise disappeared. That was seen as the Big Leap Forwards in fidelity, and in some ways it was; it democratised recording and changed listeners' notions of what fidelity had been all along – relative. Prior to digital, you rarely heard a record that included any sounds that were deliberately compromised; now it's common to hear lo-fi, or even purposely nasty sounds used as an effect or feature in an otherwise pristine mix. So much so, that listeners don't discriminate about sound in the way they used to – lo-fi, mid-fi, hi-fi – anything is equally acceptable, as long as it's effective and appropriate to the context in which it's placed. That's very liberating. It makes it possible for a record made in the most humble circumstances to compete with and be as valid as any big league blockbuster. The only difference between them is the size of the promo budget. And it makes the analogue vs digital debate redundant – it all just depends what it is.

In home studios, 24bit/44.1kHz is the most commonly used resolution at the time of writing. Some of you may opt for 24/48kHz (it's a *Mac* thing), or, like commercial facilities, may prefer 32bit/96kHz and upward, However, it's questionable whether this is warranted just yet, considering that it will likely be dithered down – with the attendant resolution loss – on most playback platforms and domestic equipment. You can lose more than you gain.

All that being said, I've nothing against 16bit for recording, then rendering the mixes at 24/44.1; admittedly, I run obsolete computers. The bigger

difference is really in the quality of the A/D converters in your computer/interface. Poorer ones will sound thin and brittle. In that event, there's not much you can do other than change your system, or live with it and compensate as best you can.

Fidelity is relative; one person may gravitate to the mathematical precision of Bach, another, a Turkish punk band. You wouldn't necessarily want to record them both the same way and fidelity – as most commonly accepted – is more important to one than the other. Actually, it just has to be as sympathetic as possible to what's being recorded. Once you've got rid of the 60Hz ground loop, noise and crackles, fidelity is only limited to your equipment and how well or appropriately you use it. You can dither all you like about bit rates, when playback is through a 1in computer speaker. Either way, the listener is more interested in the tune, or the people playing it. You could argue that if fidelity mattered that much, we'd never hear anything made prior to 1996.

I've made more than one record where I've deliberately left in all the snap, crackles and pop. Not one person – including recording engineers – has ever pulled me up on it. As long as it represents the project in the best possible way with the equipment available, you've got nothing to worry about.

That being said, I was mastering a new single for The Pretty Things a few years back. The A side was a new, digitally recorded live recording, while the B side was a hitherto unreleased track from the early 1960s, taken from an acetate. For you younger readers, acetates were one-off, one-sided vinyl test pressings, with a very limited life. After a few plays, the thin plastic outer layer began to wear out and the record got very scratchy and crackly. This particular acetate had had its share of plays over the years and before I even heard it, I knew it couldn't be restored completely. No matter – the song was great, the performance full of energy and the recording itself very well made.

What struck me as I listened, was how the

crackles, static and noise added a very definite sense of time and place that would not be at all evident in an antiseptically clean, overly enhanced, digitised remaster. It set me thinking: how best to reconcile this with the newly recorded A-side song, when there was such a huge sonic divide between them?

It was obvious – and completely contrary to the precepts of mastering – add crackles, pops and scratches, static and noise to the *clean* track! So I looped up some vinyl gubbins from the run-out groove, mixed it on to the new recording and what do you know – it matched up with the B side and the whole thing sounded like a record!

This was the kind of conceptually sound, if technically questionable, idea that I come up with from time to time and hope to get away with. I liked it, at any rate. Only then did the label tell me that the single was a prequel for a new live album, so, promotionally, putting scratches on the A side was not exactly the best idea … I wish they had told me that in the first place!

2
PRE-PRODUCTION

RECORDISTS, ENGINEERS AND PRODUCERS

So far, we've established that you already have, or are intending to have, a recording studio of some kind; you're a recordist, an engineer, or a producer, perhaps. Let's define those roles more clearly. As purely a recordist, you're self-contained. You might be a musician recording yourself, or just interested in sound and what you can do with it. Probably you're not thinking of running a commercial facility, though you might be interested in releasing your own recordings. You alone will be responsible for making all the decisions about the creative or technical aspects of the recordings from start to finish. Everything is on your shoulders, but in some ways, that's easier.

Engineers traditionally are part of a team and do all the technical stuff. They make sure that everything works as it should, for the people they work with. They know where to plug things in, place the microphones, how to operate the equipment and put a reasonable mix together in a short space of time. They might run their own studio, or work for someone who does. Their relationship with the people they work with is just as important as the technical skills they have. Engineers are not record producers, the main difference being that it's their clients who make the creative decisions (*or think they do*).

The impression most people have about record producers is that they're the people behind the glass, who tell everyone what to do. Certainly, they're responsible to the artists and companies they work for in delivering the final recording to everyone's satisfaction, but it's also a collabora-

tive role and this is often overlooked, whether it's plugging the gaps, fixing a song, or suggesting new ideas.

There are many wannabes who wrongly think of themselves as producers. Sometimes it's an ego trip about getting their name on the record, or lending 'authority' to themselves because they feel entitled to do so for funding a project. In reality, you work up to being a producer when you have enough musical and/or technical nous to warrant it. You're involved from start to finish, sometimes long before you get as far as stepping inside a studio.

Most producers start out as recording engineers, musicians, or songwriters, and every producer has their own style. They might be hands on with every detail, or focus entirely on the sounds and performance, or be fundamentally enablers, inspiring their artists to discover and excel. A producer need not be a skilled musician, or a tech whizz, but must have vision. The more comprehensive their knowledge of musical forms and understanding of how to create and manipulate sound, the better. As a producer, you need to be insightful, honest, but tactful (and sometimes not!). The artist has to take your word for it that everything will be okay.

STUDIO DYNAMICS

The working dynamic of a session tends to be – like it or not – (1) producer, (2) engineer, (3) artist. Most engineers understand this intuitively and producers exploit it for the good of the project. Though the engineer is a sort-of second in command, they are essential to a successful recording, not just technically, but in their unique position as a buffer between the producer and the artist. Artists intrinsically see engineers as an ally. If they feel intimidated by a producer's experience or manner, they will gravitate towards the engineer for reassurance and as a conduit by which a producer can be persuaded (though this is not necessarily true!). This artist/engineer dynamic is invaluable and a skilled producer knows it, letting the engineer offer support and input as needed. An engineer doesn't criticise and is seen as impartial; the producer is where the buck stops and must always play devil's advocate, asking for yet another take, pointing out that the guitar needs tuning, or coaxing a great performance. The artist can all too easily feel they're at the bottom of the food chain … but remember that without them, there would be no project!

An engineer is often given a producer's role by default when there is no 'producer' involved. It's not unusual for a band to book a studio and be under the impression that the engineer will be producing the session, but only in the sense of getting a good result. They seriously expect that an engineer, who has never heard them before, will be able to deliver a pristine, radio-ready mix, without the opportunity for any prior input about the project. Inevitably they will be disappointed, book a different studio next time and repeat the same mistake elsewhere.

It's not out of the ordinary to be both engineer and producer. That's a bigger weight to carry, but there are positive aspects to it. You tend to have a closer relationship with the artist and often end up working with them in the long term – you become integral to what they do.

PRODUCING YOURSELF

Working on your own projects will be the most demanding. Everyone is more precious when it's their own thing, understandably so. But you still have to step back far enough to see all the strengths and all the weaknesses. If you don't, you'll be liable to be going round in circles before you know it.

While you can't completely detach yourself, you can still be analytical and take every sound on its own merits. Imagine it was someone else's work. What would you tell them? You have to be brutal sometimes. When a piece you thought wonderful at the time doesn't seem so hot after the fact, you have to be honest with yourself and take it on the chin. Use the same yardstick as you would for anyone else and ask the same questions; is that intro too long, that guitar part appropriate, the sixteenth keyboard overdub really overkill?

It's great to try as many things as you're inspired to do, as long as you can mercilessly weed them out afterwards. Don't be too much of a perfectionist. You'll overwork the project and it will sound like it. Be disciplined. You can have lots of fun and amuse yourself with clever tech or musical tricks – but the average listener won't pick up on them or be interested anyway. Mostly, you need to be objective when you're producing your own recordings or pet projects. But no matter how dispassionate you can be, there will be times when your perspective is lost.

If you have a crisis of confidence, play what you're working on to someone else. They may not know much, but can certainly tell you if the drums are too loud. When you produce yourself, it's not the details that are difficult, but the simple, obvious things that are likely to trip you up.

BRAINSTORMING

When you're embarking on a new project, whether it's your own or in collaboration, right at the start you will have at least a rough idea of what it might turn out to be; even just the obvious things – the style, the likely instruments it will have – you know, the basics.

Taking some time to really think about what you're planning to do has a real, lasting impact on every aspect of the project. The way you imagine

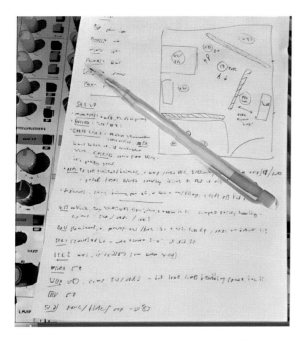

Session work sheet includes sketch of mic and baffle placement.

what a recording should be like when it's done dictates the choices you make about how to get there, so look at the nuts and bolts and join the dots together. All the components are interrelated, in a miniature ecosystem of sound – if you want to be cosmic about it. But this is also practical stuff. The more detail you go into, the more you realise it's all about the relationships between sounds. Are they compatible with one another, or will they disagree? Harmony, balance, dynamics and structure are the elements you have to play with. Look deeply into your little universe of sound – will the planets align, or disappear down a black hole?

Start with the broadest brushstrokes, then work down to the finer details. You may only have sign-posts to begin with; it's up to you to discover the correct address.

So do some brainstorming. Take a blank sheet of paper and write down, as randomly as you like, everything you can think of or associate with the project. Just jot down whatever it is that comes into your head, whether it makes sense or not. Let

your mind wander freely and try to go beyond your conscious thoughts.

What's the use of a bit of free association, you may ask – but more than you expect will be relevant in some way or another and will definitely give you insights that you didn't have before. If you don't know what the record is about, or really wondered what it should be, this will help you to find out. Do what the record asks. You can interpret it in different ways, but can't make it into something it's not. Starting a recording without a framework is pointless – and is not improvising. Improvising relies on having something on which to improvise!

Right from the start, I always thought of what I did in terms of finished records, simply because that was my objective. So I'd work on songs with a view to them being part of an EP, or an album, or a single. Something as simple as that gave me a roadmap to follow, with defined boundaries and a definite beginning, middle and end. I'd group twelve songs together for an album, which by default gives you a feeling for light and shade, side one and side two, which kind of track would fit here or there in a running order – form and dimension. There was always a concept to work from and fulfil, which is in itself inspiring. I'd go the whole hog and make sleeve designs to send out with the tapes, with a clear purpose in mind.

In retrospect, I can see now how valuable this was. Whatever I imagined, I tried to do with the tools that were available; because there was only one mic, I learned a lot about placement and balancing sounds. I wasn't able to overdub with my tape recorder, so I brought in extra musicians as needed, everything from drums, to cellos or French horns. Once, even a bicycle – for the bell, you see. I just followed the picture I had in my head of what the record wanted to be. I still do that now.

SONG PYRAMID

Now, you've recovered from journeying into the farthest corners of your mind, the studio is set up and you're all plugged in and ready to do some recording. It's time to do a little bit of preparation before you wade in and press the red button. The success of the final recording will be in direct proportion to the effectiveness of your pre-production.

The first time you assess material for a new recording is the most important, as it's the only occasion when it will be completely fresh to your ears. Take notes as you go about the direction, feel, strong points and weaknesses. Problems with structure will be most apparent on first hearing and serve as a good indicator of the ease or complexity of the job in hand. Strictly speaking, songs and musical arrangements are the province of musicians or producers, but even if you are a recordist or engineer, it's useful to have some insights into how they work, as they have a significant effect on the results of a recording and you may be looked to for opinions and suggestions from time to time.

The structure of the musical – or unmusical – material has to work as seamlessly and effectively as possible, preferably before you record it. Music ebbs and flows melodically and rhythmically to keep the listener interested and involved from start to finish, and songs in particular have a common structural form. The bones of a song are built like a pyramid. The pinnacle is equivalent to the main idea or feeling that's being conveyed; typically, the chorus or hook line. The only reason for other parts of a song to exist at all is to support this main theme. Everything leading up to it should create anticipation and everything leading away, resolution. If this tension and release is compromised, all the focal points will be weaker for it.

Structural problems mostly tend to occur in the transitions between verse to chorus, chorus to verse, in bridge sections and intros. Writers often try to write themselves out of poor transitions by adding extra bridges, which compounds the problem further, failing to recognise that simply deleting a few bars may have been the answer all along.

Always look to simple subtractive editing, or moving sections of a song around to fix weak structures. Intros are invariably too long and can usually be halved. Or they completely lack impact – if I hear another eight-bar, two-chord, solo rhythm guitar opening, I swear I will stick my head in a bucket. Intros with a different rhythmic pattern or tempo from the rest of the song always feel out of place and should be axed. In fact, time-signature changes as a rule are clumsy except for all but the most experienced, and should be made consistent.

Dispose of any superfluous bridge sections or instrumental solos and make sure that the song gets to the chorus fast enough – within 30 seconds

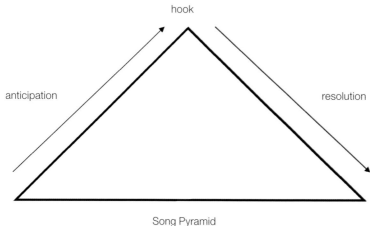

hook

anticipation

resolution

Song Pyramid

The song pyramid.

Ready and waiting.

Song Structure

A standard kind of song structure looks like this:

- **intro / verse / chorus / verse / chorus / bridge / verse / chorus / chorus / outro.**

Or this:

- **intro / chorus / verse / chorus / bridge / verse / chorus / chorus / outro.**

You can see how the different parts are almost interchangeable.

if you want any airplay. If it doesn't, suggest adding an additional chorus or instrumental version of it, right at the beginning. Tightening up structures really helps.

MUSICAL ARRANGEMENTS

Records made in the early 1960s relied heavily on very tightly worked-out arrangements. With only four tracks (and sometimes only two) available, overdubs were often reserved just for vocals. The better the musical arrangement, the less you have to worry about micing up, mixing, or anything else. It's hard trying to get a good mix out of a crummy arrangement. The main problem area with bands is that habitually everyone plays all the way through the song, all the time. That's fine for a gig, but recordings need a well-defined, strong dynamic structure, with development, contrast and continual focal points to keep things interesting throughout repeated listenings. So parts have to be worked out carefully and be sympathetic to the other instruments that are playing. If the basics don't work, no amount of overdubbing will fix it. This is not a gig, it's a record, and that has different requirements.

The basics of an arrangement consist of instruments that play all, or most, of the time – drums, bass and rhythm guitar. They need to be rhythmi-cally cohesive, with all the key structural points of the song clearly apparent.

Developing the arrangement from there isn't just a case of piling more stuff on top as the song progresses. Let's say that verse two is identical to verse one, so needs development. You don't necessarily have to add something else. Iinterest could be kept going without any overdubs, simply by one or more of the basic instruments changing their parts slightly, such as moving root notes or chords under the melody, or making subtle rhythmic changes. Look to the development of parts before considering overdubs, unless a specific overdub had been decided on and prepared prior to recording. Off the cuff layering of overdubs is seldom effective. There is always a tendency for musicians to overplay, so keep a tight rein on the parts!

Other than the core instrumentation, overdubs will be in and out at specific cue points, often one handing off to another. They are there to add colour, maintain interest and create focal points that give sonic cues of anticipation and resolution to the listener. A drum fill leading into a chorus has this kind of function. More often than not, there will be too many overdub ideas, which need to be weeded out and combined into a practical layout. Justify each and every note – the fewer dubs, the better. And be sure that none of the parts conflict with, or unduly distract from the lead vocal.

Two Fingers

To portray a real instrument convincingly using samples or keyboard presets, approach it as though you were playing the instrument in question, or it will not seem authentic. It's not enough to reproduce texture and sound; the type of part the instrument would naturally play should also be reproduced. Ask yourself 'What is this instrument's natural range?' and don't play outside of it. How many notes can be played at once on it? Don't exceed the maximum.

Think harmony and counterpoint when constructing string, brass or woodwind parts – not chords. For example, cellos rarely play more than two of their four strings at once, so restricting yourself to a maximum of two notes at a time not only sounds more true, it helps in working out an appropriate part. A string quartet done in this way on a keyboard would have a two-finger part representing cello and viola, plus another for the pair of violins.

Mapping an Arrangement

Once the arrangement is complete (or almost complete – there may well be a few things you can't pin down just yet), make a map of it. It might look something like this:

- **intro: drums, piano, bass**
- **verse one: drums, piano, bass, lead vocal**
- **chorus one: drums, piano, bass, guitar, lead vocal, double-track vocal**
- **verse two: drums, piano, bass, guitar, organ, lead vocal**
- **chorus two: drums, piano, bass, guitar, lead vocal, double-track vocal**
- **bridge: drums, piano, bass, guitar, organ, trumpet solo, backing vocal (BV) 1, BV2, BV3, BV4 (la-las)**
- **chorus three: drums, piano, bass, guitar, lead vocal, double-track vocal**
- **outro: drums, piano, bass.**

You will note that just looking at the map, the structure, symmetry and dynamics are apparent in the arrangement, as is the pinnacle of the song pyramid – unusually in this case, during the bridge.

The arrangement is the core of your mix and it's better to make decisions now than wonder how on earth to make it all work later. Remember, the space between notes is every bit as important as the notes themselves; use it to your advantage. Watch out not only for the clutter of too many notes, but for rhythmic conflicts between instruments, which always sound awkward. Be sure that the phrasing of the lead vocal is sitting comfortably.

The symmetry of an arrangement should be evident in the structure and instrumentation. For example, lead guitar licks may be featured on the intro, bridge and outro, but you would be unlikely to hear them in verse or chorus one and nowhere else. These kinds of focal points often carry the main theme, or variations of it. Feature instruments create highlights other than the lead vocal, so there is always a new point of interest, or sense of momentum.

SCHEDULING

It's useful to make a guesstimate of the length of time that might be required for a given session, to make the most efficient use of it and to give structure and direction to any recording, whether you're an engineer, producer, or musician.

WORKING OUT SESSION TIMINGS

When recording a band, allow at least an hour for them to set up and get focused. Keep an eye on them to make sure they don't get distracted and start chatting, making more tea, going to the shop, collecting their washing, that sort of thing. They'll be tuning and warming up another fifteen minutes after that before they're ready for a run-through. Record the run-through, but don't tell them. It's the only chance you'll have to capture an unselfconscious performance, where no one is worried about making a mistake – because it's a run-through, right? It's not unknown for the feel of the run-through to excel and it may just be a case of a few mix adjustments, or an odd punch-in to fix any errors (which you'll find yourself doing regardless of which take is best).

If the band is tight, they may well be able to retake entire sections of a song, which can be edited together later, such as a loose ending, or intro. This is a very old-school technique, still typical with orchestras; record two complete takes of a piece and use one to edit out the mistakes of the other. Orchestras are expensive, so you can't have them hanging around for a moment longer than necessary! When The Beatles discovered performances could be edited, they seldom did anything else, to the point of leaving deliberate blank spaces on backing tracks for parts of songs that hadn't been written yet!

Typical Tight Schedule for a Rock Band Single Session

Day One
7:00–10:00pm   Take two to three hours to set up mics, get basic sounds and let the musicians get the feel of the studio.

Day Two
10:00–11:00am   Fine-tune set-up and sounds while the musicians wake up.

11:00am–2:00pm   Record basic tracks and any repairs needed to them.

2:00–2:30pm   Lunch. Musicians can take a little longer, so make sure the one you need next for overdubs is prompt!

2:30–4:45pm   Three guitar overdubs.

4:45–6:15pm   Two keyboard dubs.

6:15–9:15pm   Vocals.

9:15–10:00pm   One percussion overdub (in reality, it will take twenty minutes for the dub and twenty-five minutes for everyone to pack up their bits and pieces before they leave).

If ahead at this point, add time to the following day. A spare hour for mixing never does any harm. If behind, a simple last overdub can be done quickly at the start of tomorrow's session.

Day Three
10:00am–1:00pm   Basic mix set-up.

1:00–1:30pm   Lunch.

1:30–3:30pm   Mix A side.

3:30–4:00pm   Break.

4:00–7:00pm   Mix B side.

7:00–8:00pm   Allowance for downtime, submixes and copying.

But back to scheduling. A band playing together will manage three takes without a break. That's three times the song length to record, another three times the song length to listen to the takes – and another five minutes more for discussion, after they've completed all three. Stop them from performing an autopsy on each take right after they've finished it, or they'll take forever getting back into the groove. Aim for take two to begin as soon as take one has faded away and stay in record mode.

Any subsequent takes after the first three will be one at a time and much slower going. Take a short break after a band has finished live tracking; everyone will need a breather by then. Allow thirty minutes. Maximum. It will always turn into 45.

Overdubs are where the time goes. Musicians often overestimate their abilities, get anxious with everyone watching them, make lots of timing and phrasing errors, as well as more obvious mistakes, then make more mistakes because they're embarrassed about making them. This is because it's not that easy to rehearse overdubs or remember parts and not something they do every day. It will take roughly ten minutes to set up for each group of overdubs. If possible, do all guitar overdubs on all the songs before moving on to all the keyboard dubs, the vocals and so on, rather than adding all the overdubs on one song before moving on to the next.

You can expect to achieve three instrumental overdubs in an hour. This may seem like a generous amount of time, but in fact it's quite intense in practice. It keeps up the momentum, stops over-analysing and gives you a buffer for tricky parts that the band might get stuck on. Lead vocals will take approximately one and a half hours for the average vocalist, though a good one will be a lot faster. Allow a similar amount of time for backing vocals.

You can estimate, on average, forty-five minutes to an hour for each backing track, instrumental or backing vocal overdub, then an hour for an easy lead vocal, but three hours for a tough one. Playbacks eat into session time and break the musicians' concentration. Only allow them when you're confident takes are complete.

Running a tight, efficient session is in everybody's interest; the less wasted time, the better. Record while everyone is still fresh and focused – once people are tired, it's a law of diminishing returns. By working out a time schedule, you'll be able to estimate realistically the total hours needed in advance. Here's a typical tight schedule for a rock-band single session.

A more relaxed schedule for the same session would be split over three eight-hour days (again with set-up time prior to the session), combining basic tracks with some overdubbing on day two, remaining overdubs and basic mix set-up on day three, and A and B mixes completed on day four.

The Telescopes Session

To demonstrate the advantages of planning ahead of a recording session, you may find it enlightening to read the notes I made for myself prior to recording The Telescopes; there are details on the mic choices, a thorough schedule and even adjustments to the monitoring and compression settings. These are the actual notes I made, vertabim, with all my typos and abbreviations left in.

MONITORS

Last time I rolled of −2dB on bass and added +½dB his to the adam spkrs. That was close, but mix was too bassy and lacking esp in hi mids. They tend to compress the sound, so too flattering. Next TIME maybe just roll off −1dB bass?

MONITORING *would prefer no headphones, they play well in live environment—but see what they prefer; possibly for bass if spillt is problem; reamp it later as Jim suggested*

If no hphones, **need spkr for talkback**.

KRK monitors—bassy; roll off some; have boost/cut switches on back. Adjust amp if not enough.

TEST TRACKS :—mc Cartney that would be something for monitoring accuracy

BAND REF live vid 'I remember everything' good sound = no overdubs needed, and very little other than balancing.

MICS

Kit

OHs —]**MK012s which capsules?**

kick— / 421/audix D6/57/ e 906 *whichever is deepest with some punch*

Snare beyer m201/57/

Also liked ribbon in front idea, though don't know if it will work in this configuration—in front of the kit, the same distance from the snare as the overheads.

Bass—

e906/**421** *need deep, widescreen bass sound*

Gtr/kbd cabs 57/**sm7** *lead gtr needs good tonal range*

Vox — sm7/ 421/m201 / ribbon *if pitched low*

SCHEDULE

8-hr day

Day One

10:30–11:30 set up

11:30–12:30 track 1 **keep playing unless I say stop!**

12:30–1:30 track 2

1:30–2:00 retakes / editing if needed

2:00–3:00 vox dubs
3:00–4:00 gtr dubs
4:00–5:00 other dubs
5:00–6:00 allowance for estimated time used during day for breaks/playbacks etc

Day Two
10:30–11:30 mix set up * note desk wired in AFTER interfaces so watch settings
11:30–2:00 mix 1
2:30–4:30 mix 2
4:30–5:30 allowance for edits/whatever
5:30–6:30 export wavs mixes + multitrack
MIX I think they're running Logic Pro, in which case compressors are
great; if Pro Tools, use silver and black compressors.

Logic Pro compressors –
vintage opto = la2a
studio vca = fovusrite red
,
vintage vca
thr -10 , rat 2.25, make up 10.5, knee 0.7, attack 10,rel 50 auto gain -12,
input/output settings 0

vintage opto;
thr -20.1, rat 2, make up 6, knee 7, at 10, rel 50
or
thr -38 rat 3 makeup -5 knee 0.8 at 18 rel 48

studio vca;
thr 15 rat 2 makeup 0 auto gain on at 10 rel 50

In reality, I'd *overestimated* the time that was needed. The band were terrific, tracking was fast, mixes took
half the time I'd expected and we wrapped up around lunchtime on day two. *Keep playing unless I say stop!*

3
RECORDING

Recording can be a hugely rewarding experience, whether you're out front or behind the desk. I'm at my best when I feel like I *almost* know what I'm doing. So don't be intimidated by it – it's good to be intuitive. Aim to get as close to the finished sound as you can by your choice and positioning of microphones.

Put the mics in the right place and it will give you a faithful representation of the performance. Easy as that? Not quite – you have to use your best judgment on how any particular sound will work with all the others that surround it in the mix. It helps immensely when you have a clear picture in your mind of all the sounds that will be in the final recording (well, around 80 per cent of them, you're

allowed some room for inspiration!). Nothing is in isolation; try to imagine how everything will work together.

So what *will* the finished record be like? Write down, track by track, all the components and sounds you think you will need. That will tell you how to proceed, which mics to use and in what order things should be done. You can practise this with your favourite records. Listen to them, take them apart in your head, note what you think has been used on each track, how the sounds were used – and the things you couldn't figure out. This trains you to identify sounds and the way they affect one another. It's always full of surprises.

Taking a Record Apart

The following method shows you how to take a record apart in order to identify its various sounds. To start with, pick a record from your collection, then write down notes as you go.

First, listen to the drums and bass – focus on them, concentrate and do your best to ignore all the other sounds in the mix. How do they relate to one another? What is the balance like between them? Is the kick or the bass the dominant one? How loud is the snare in comparison?

Then, turn your attention to the main rhythmic instruments – guitars or keyboards. Where are they placed in relation to the drums and bass? Are there any effects on them? How are they panned?

When you've done that, move on to the feature instruments. What are they and where do they happen? What is their level in the mix? How much louder are they than the rhythmic instruments?

Lastly, focus on the vocals. Are they more prominent than you expected? What kind of reverb was used? A long reverb, a short one, or with a delay added behind it? How would you describe the compression? Is it heavy or light? Are there any special effects you don't recognise?

What is it about this record that you like the most? Why did you choose it? Is there anything that doesn't work, or that you would change, or didn't understand? What surprised you? Listen again and see what you missed the first time. There are songs I must have heard hundreds of times, but still discover new things in them. Great records will do that to you.

MANAGING TRACKS

Back in the olden days of recording, when everything was live in the studio, engineers would ride fader levels and cues in real time during the recording itself. It was the only way to mix and balance the microphones. I say microphones – all of them were recorded on to one mono track, with any effects required applied to them. That takes a lot of skill and a penchant for living dangerously. They didn't call them Balance Engineers for nothing. I'm not suggesting you try that, but I can offer some options to make recording with digital a little less complicated.

On your digital platform, you're working either completely 'in the box', with just a stereo input for recording, or you have an interface allowing you to record four or more tracks at the same time, possibly with faders. Some of you may even have interfaced an analogue mixer with your system. The same principles apply regardless, the only difference being the number of tracks at your disposal.

Sadly, some software programs encourage the user to open a new track, rather than punch in on the same one to repair errors while recording, which can be unnecessarily difficult and counterintuitive. The trouble is, if you're opening new tracks every time you make a repair, you end up with sixty plus tracks to wade through at mixdown. And managing sixty tracks is not easy for cross-referencing, balancing levels, or anything else for that matter. When there are no limits on the number of tracks you can use, there's a temptation to save each and every take, instead of weeding out the duff tones as you go – and before you know it, you're asking 'Is track nineteen better than track thirty-four?'…'Hang on, let's check it again …'. After several tortuous hours, the conclusion is that take one was in fact the keeper.

Quick and decisive decisions are best. Multiple choices made after the fact are harder than those done in the moment and it will be difficult to match the feel and balance levels evenly when you have thirty alternates piled up in front of you. It makes so much more sense to make those decisions as you record. If you've found it's more convenient with your software to open a new track than continue recording on the same one, you might want to switch to another program. Audacity's free program includes a 'punch and roll' feature, while current versions of Pro Tools and Logic offer a 'quick punch' facility.

Keeping the total track count to a minimum is really important in streamlining the workflow of both the recording and mixing process, regardless of the platform you use. By recording a complete take on the main track and punching in on it as needed to repair errors or glitches at the time, before moving on to the next track, you won't spend hours sifting through all those outtakes when you mix. You will have a complete performance – which is what you were aiming for in the first place, wasn't it?

There are just four straightforward steps:

1. **Record** a complete take.
2. **Select** region to repair.
3. **Perform** the punch-in.
4. **Listen** and check that the repair matches in feel and volume.

Save as you go when you record. Discard poor takes and keep only one alternate if there's a good reason, such as if it has a different feel, or perhaps for use later as a double track. If you're brave and have an effect you really like, save it as an alternate with the effect on – you may not be able to duplicate it precisely later. The fewer tracks you use, the easier it is to compare and reference their relationships in context with each other.

MICING UP

There are an infinite number of ways you can position microphones, some tried and tested, others unorthodox and surprising. 'Put it where it sounds right' is exactly so; but you have to recog-

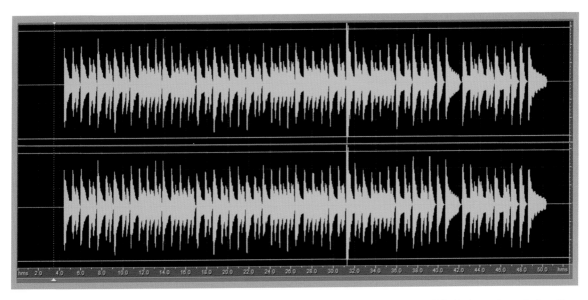

Record a complete take, or record until making an error; whatever works best for you. This will likely depend on whether it's a main track, or an overdub.

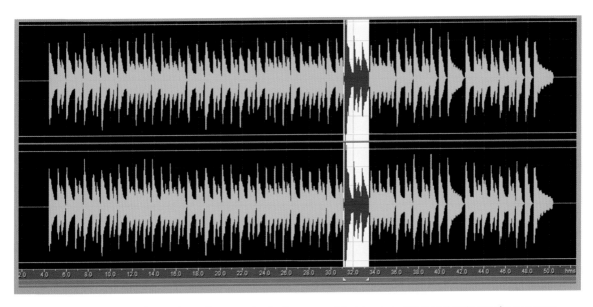

Select punch-in points to make repairs on the same track after a complete take, or punch in and make repairs as you go.

nise when it sounds good and that is arguably the hardest part.

You could begin with a typical position; maybe a microphone right up on the cone of a guitar amplifier. Many may think this is bulletproof. It isn't. The variables are the room, the amplifier, the guitar,

the guitarist and the type of mic you are using. A mic on the cone might be satisfactory, but moving it further away could be better. You won't know unless you try it and compare.

What are you looking for? Should it be loud and punchy, or subtle and sweet? You're not just trying to find a 'good' sound – you want the right sound that will work for the mix you have in mind. Is the amplifier set to the correct tone and volume? In which part of the room does it sound most convincing? At what distance is the 'throw' of the amplifier? Is there spillage likely from other instruments? How does it affect the sound when it's in context with them? Consider all these factors before you stick a mic in front of the amplifier.

My own introduction to recording was with a mono tape recorder and a single microphone, which I attached to an old anglepoise lamp for an improvised stand. There was no information available then about recording, or recording schools, or anything else; you were completely left to your own devices. The only book I ever found on the subject at the time was by songwriter Tony Hatch. It had a diagram of a mixing desk in it, showing a channel strip with all its knobs and faders, and he tried to explain how changing one sound would affect everything else. I was completely mystified. Hell, I didn't even know anyone who owned a bass guitar.

Fortunately, I was used to figuring out things for myself. I'd listen, and position the mic to balance the instruments where they were, if possible, but that was limited to the 2m (6.5ft) cable length of the mic; so the musicians, amplifiers and so on would often need to be moved around to accommodate where the *microphone* was. I'd just run a test take or two and check what it sounded like to get the best out of it. It doesn't take long when you don't have much equipment! I think the most instruments recorded at one time were drums, guitar, vocals, backing vocals, organ, two cellos and percussion. It all seemed simple and intuitive, really – and worked surprisingly well. We'd get two or three songs done in a session and only kept the best takes. Tape was expensive, so you recorded over it. The point is, it doesn't matter how little you have at your disposal. As long as you know what you want and use your ears, it will work.

This 'close your eyes and point' technique is relevant and, in my opinion, the best starting point you can have. It trains you to listen closely and to

Try This on for Size

A lone microphone may sound too simple for words, but it provides a great lesson in mic placement. You can record virtually any combination of instruments with one microphone. The results depend on the room you're in, the mic and recorder, and the skill of the musicians.

Try this on for size; set the musicians up in a way that's comfortable for them. A semicircle or variation of one usually works well. The musicians should play at a volume level that is not excessive, with no one instrument predominant. Armed with your microphone of choice (a cardioid, or omnidirectional, is the most versatile), put on your favourite headphones to monitor the signal of the mic. The headphones should be loud enough so that you can distinguish the mic from the external sound in the room. Or challenge yourself and don't use headphones at all – just listen and point the microphone where your ears tell you to.

Holding the mic at ear height, a little in front of your face, stand at a central point between or in front of the musicians, close your eyes and slowly turn your head back and forth, up and down. The balance and tone of the instruments will change as the mic moves with you. Listen carefully. You will find a place where the balance and tone between the instruments feels most even and natural. Open your eyes, note the mic position, put it on its stand in that spot and listen again. Now adjust and refine the position – very small movements will make a difference. If a particular instrument is too quiet or too loud, have the musician move back or forwards from the mic, or adjust their volume if amplified. With a modest mic, in a reasonably decent room, you'll be surprised at how good the results can be.

hear subtle changes in sonics and balance. But some established guidelines and reference points are useful.

MICROPHONE PLACEMENT

Remember this; sound travels from the source and through the air before reaching your ears. The airspace is important in determining the definition and dimension of a recording. Placing a mic right onto an instrument or vocalist, only 2.5cm (1in) or so away, will sound the most contained and upfront. The farther away you move it, the more open it becomes, as you play with the airspace; the reflections in the room (reverb) change the tonal values and perceived distance. The mic placement you decide upon depends on the result you're aiming for.

I can't give you precise details of exactly where to put microphones, as the sound of your room, the mics you've got, the signal chain and the players will vary. But the positions described are an accurate guide as to what will work in most situations. Let's call them *almost* bulletproof. Your ears have to be the judge and you should adjust, experiment and adapt the placements as you see fit.

DRUMS

There are more questions about how to mic up drums than anything else, ever. Recordists worry themselves sick about what microphones to use. Is this one better than that one? Do I compress them or not? How should the kit be tuned? What day of the week is it? The list just grows … The most common misconception is that in order to record drums correctly, each individual drum must have a separate microphone and track. In effect, this means reassembling the natural sound of the kit at the mixing stage, which can be anything but straightforward and, most of the time, fairly pointless. I will concentrate on some simpler methods.

Before micing up a drum kit, make sure that it is set up with enough room to position mics anywhere around it, preferably with enough ceiling height to accommodate mics at least 60cm (2ft) above the cymbals. You can work with less; it just limits your options a bit. We work with what we've got.

Wear headphones whilst positioning the mics to find the optimum sonic and balance, make a test recording or two and check it on your monitors, so that you can then pinpoint any adjustments that need to be made.

MINIMAL DRUM-KIT MICING

A drum kit is one, unified instrument. Lots of mics panned unnaturally will not balance well and will sound artificial, even in talented hands. You wouldn't mic each note of a piano and try to put it together later, would you?

I've always taken the easy way out and used as few mics as possible on drums, never more than four. Over the years I've found that to be most effective – let alone indispensable when time is of the essence. My favourite technique was devised by Glyn Johns in the late 1960s and used on his work with The Beatles, The Rolling Stones, The Who and Led Zeppelin (yes, *that* Led Zeppelin sound). Basically, it's a three-mic method, using two overhead microphones, another on the kick and an optional fourth 'just in case' mic on the snare. The innovative nature of placing an overhead looking across the floor tom was allegedly accidental – but Mr Johns knows his engineering science well. Just follow the simple instructions and it will always work.

You'll need a tape measure, two condenser microphones for overheads and two dynamics: one for the kick, another for the fourth, optional, snare mic.

1. Position the first overhead between 75cm–1.5m (2.5–5ft) above the middle of the snare (exact height will vary according to your ceiling height). Listen; it should give a pretty well-balanced image of the whole kit.

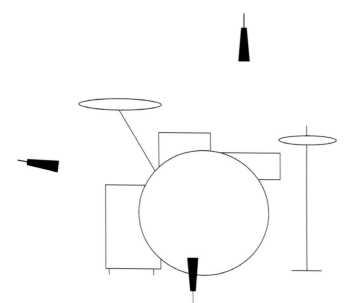

The Glyn Johns array.

Overhead mics
equidistant at 1.5m (5ft),
kick mic outside front
skin.

Kick mic on beater side.

Overheads in restricted space adapted to 60cm (2ft) equidistant, with kick mic inside shell.

2. The second overhead is placed at the same distance from the centre of the snare, a little to the right of the floor tom, roughly 10–15cm (4–6in) above the rim, looking at, and perpendicular to, the snare. It's important that the distance between the two microphones is the same.
3. Place the kick mic inside the shell, close to the beater for a tight sound, or further away for a roomier one,
4. The fourth mic is placed 5cm (2in) above the snare, pointing to the centre and angled towards the drummer.

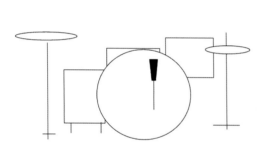

5. Pan the L/R overhead mics in the region of 10 o'clock and 2 o'clock respectively. Kick and extra snare mic are panned to centre.

There are permutations on this, depending on the drummer, the height of the cymbals and use of the floor tom. I've reduced the overhead measurements to as little as 60cm (2ft) and used only the floor tom mic for the entire kit on more than one occasion.

TWO MICROPHONES

At Abbey Road, Ringo's kit in the early 1960s was recorded with two large diaphragm condenser mics, with one overhead microphone facing downwards, placed at chin level in front of the drummer. The second, kick-drum mic is positioned roughly 15cm (6in) from the face of the bass drum, at 1 o'clock (you may need to adjust this, dependent on the mic you use).

LEFT: Ringo's set-up.

BOTTOM LEFT: Kick mic in front of bass drum.

BOTTOM RIGHT: Overhead mic at chin level.

ONE MICROPHONE

A condenser, or omnidirectional, mic works best.

Option one Place the mic a little to the right of the floor tom, roughly 10–15cm (4–6in) above the rim, looking at the snare. The drummer's body acts as a baffle to lessen the relative volume of the hi hat.

Option two Mic is placed 1.25–2m (4–6.5ft) away from the kit, pointed towards drummer's chin.

Option three Position the mic in front of the drum kit, at chest height to the drummer, roughly 60cm (2ft) away from the kick drum. Move the mic forward into the kit, or backwards, away from it, until the drums come into the right focus and balance.

Option four When Charlie Watts recorded with the Stones at Muscle Shoals Studio, a single mic was positioned on the kit directly in front of the top rim of the kick drum, 5–10cm (2–4in) away.

DRUM-KIT RECORDING TIPS

The Drummer

A drummer must keep solid timing. If he can't, he'll have to go, simple as that; there's nothing to be done about it and no amount of trying to play with click tracks will help. Even a strong drummer makes errors, so be prepared to do a little editing after the fact now and then.

Some drummers hit hard, while others have a light touch. Both are fine, as long as they hit the drums with an even, consistent weight. A good drummer has the technique to make his kit sound as good as it possibly can (and will definitely also have a well-tuned kit). A poor drummer sounds weak and uneven no matter how well-tuned the kit and the only remedy is to compress the drums as much as possible when mixing. This will help, if not solve, the problem.

There's a tendency for musicians as a whole to overplay, which in drummers equates to busy fills and inappropriate accents on snare or kick-drum patterns. Check that the snare/kick-drum part doesn't create any rhythmic conflicts with other parts of the musical arrangement, especially the lead vocal. If things don't sit well, it's usually due to friction of this type, where two or more elements are pulling in different directions. This may not be apparent when listening to the drums in isolation, so it's advisable to check the drummer's part (and the bass player's!) with the bigger picture. Most problems in musical arrangements are a result of too many ideas with too little forethought and

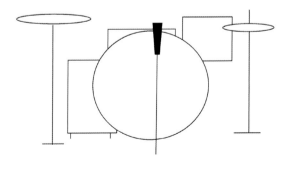

Charlie Watts's set-up.

A single mic in front of the top rim of the kit drum.

it rarely does any harm to subtract from them. Simplicity always works.

Tuning

A drum kit needs to be tuned correctly. Surprisingly, some drummers don't know how to do this, so it often falls to the recording engineer or producer to take care of it. What kind of sound should the kit have? Tight and high, like a jazz kit, tight and low for rock, or loose for a mid-sixties sound? Whatever the choice, the kit must be tonally balanced in itself.

Each drum is tuned individually and in the same way. Start with the snare drum. Release the snares from the head before tuning it. You'll see that the drumhead is attached by a series of lugs with screw heads around the rim, which, when tightened or loosened, change the pitch. Take a drumstick and tap lightly next to one of the lugs, then the one diagonally across from it, about 5cm (2in) in from the rim. Repeat this process on opposite pairs of lugs all around the drumhead. If it is in tune with itself, the tone you hear will be about the same every time. If one or more places sound higher or lower, tighten or loosen the lug until it matches the others. Check and adjust all the upper and lower drumheads in this way. Generally, it's just a matter of a little fine-tuning. When you want to change the pitch overall, you'll have to adjust every lug to the required tone.

The pitch relationship between the different drums of a kit is largely a matter of taste, but they should match tonally to form a cohesive and natural whole. The pitch difference between drums can be as little as a quarter tone, or as much as several tones, emulating a chord.

Once the kit is tuned, check for buzzes, rattles and other noises that may occur when the kit is played. Squeaky kick-drum and hi-hat pedals are commonplace, but unless very distracting, will not be noticeable in context. They are mechanical devices and never entirely quiet.

Damping

It is likely that you'll hear some unpleasant reso-

nance or ring on one or more of the drums, even though they are properly tuned, with internal dampers adjusted.

For snare and toms, place your fingertip moderately lightly on the drumhead, 5cm (2in) in from the rim and hit the drum, at 5cm (2in) intervals all the way around. You should find a place (or two) where the resonance lessens, or disappears entirely. Stick a 2.5–5cm (1–2in) strip of masking tape over that spot and hit the drum again. If the ring is still there, double up the tape and try again. You can also tape thin pieces of card of various sizes and thicknesses to the head to dampen more stubborn resonance. My own ancient, dilapidated kit was held together by bits of cigarette packets.

If you find the snares are rattling excessively, stick a piece of masking tape lightly across them to hold them more evenly to the drumhead.

A kick drum usually needs more extreme treatment, with bigger, thicker pieces of tape or card on the skin or beater and may respond better if a pillow, thick blanket, or other absorbent material is placed inside the shell. Tightening the tuning up a little can also help a lot in reducing kick-drum resonance.

For that very dead late 1960s–70s sound, drape tea towels over the snare and toms, with a thick blanket in the kick drum and the front skin of the kick drum removed. You'll be okay as long as they're still making tea towels.

ELECTRONIC DRUMS

Artificial drums have come a long way and can sound relatively naturalistic – if not real. Then again, you often hear tracks where the real drummer's playing has been so processed, edited and over-compressed to a point where it doesn't sound real either. It's all up for grabs.

Electronic drums come in all shapes and sizes, from drum machines, MIDI devices triggered by keyboards, workstation effects engines, to samples and loops. If you're hoping for a natural result, it is essential to think like a drummer when constructing patterns, so it's helpful to understand how to record a traditional drum kit, the drummer and the way that parts are constructed and played. This can be especially difficult if only some components of a full kit can be played at once, as on a computer keyboard or mouse. You'll have to constantly ask yourself 'What would a drummer do?', and watch you don't create too complex a part, or produce errors that make it feel artificial.

With MIDI-generated drums and drum machines, not only must you think carefully about how to structure the pattern, it's equally likely that you will have to balance the individual sounds in a natural way before they've even come out of the box. When balancing electronic drums, try not to make any one component too dominant. Aim for an even balance among them all. When the rest of the instruments are added, it will be far easier to identify what, if any, adjustments need to be made to the drum balance.

A few suggestions on making electronic drums more organic: if your drums are MIDI-triggered or sequenced, dequantise them. Only play parts which are humanly possible to play. A combination of 'live' playing and machine-generated parts won't generally work, so check for timing inconsistencies. Another trick in humanising drum machines – especially those with fixed patterns that can't be programmed – is to feed the sound through an external speaker and place a mic 60–80cm (2–2.6ft) away. A little air space can work wonders, when mixed into the balance.

By contrast, if you *don't* want a natural drum-kit sound, take the opposite approach and imagine how to sound *least* like a drummer. Think in terms of how few components can be used. A kick drum or hi hat may be all that's necessary, or a hi hat might be supplanted by a synth. It will also make a difference if the function of the recording is entirely rhythmic, or whether the rhythms are there to support a melodic structure.

Samples and loops of full kits will have an inbuilt sonic balance, so it's usually just a matter of layering and muting to achieve the result you're looking for. If you are using samples of each component of the drum kit, it's a bigger task to assemble.

I once had a set of samples for a Ludwig kit,

each drum painstakingly recorded for its tone, tuning, drumstick weight and anything else you could think of. There were roughly 100 different samples for every component of the kit – top and bottom snare, rack toms, floor toms, kick, plus a range of cymbals to match. How you were supposed to audition every isolated sample and decide which was best for each and in context of its companions, I couldn't tell you. Life is just too short. I bet you could mix an entire album and still have change, the amount of time it would take to set up and adjust that lot. I took a pragmatic approach and chose samples for each drum at random, the rationale being that when I put them together it was a good-sounding kit regardless. It sounded nice enough. But no matter how many hours I might have spent choosing samples, adjusting the weight of the hits, or using drummer-like fills, it still wouldn't ever sound like a real, actual person was playing it.

My point is to illustrate the extreme lengths some people are prepared to go to put human drummers out of a job. As it is, most of them are unemployed. Those who are not, are expected to play to a click, which defeats the purpose of having a living, breathing drummer in the first place. Or perhaps it illustrates how difficult it is to find a decent drummer. It is true that there *are* plenty of efficient drummers out there, but very few have that special something. And that is why many classic records feature maybe only a dozen drummers.

BASS GUITARS

Use a large dynamic, dynamic, or condenser microphone 2.5–5cm (1–2in) away from the speaker, 5–7cm (2–2.75in) from the centre of the cone. If you're using a condenser microphone without a pad switch, don't go too close, or you'll blow out the mic capsule.

Choice of strings and playing style are a major factor in determining the characteristic of an electric bass, as are the tone settings on the guitar and

Sennheiser 421 dynamic on the cone.

amplifier. Listen carefully for overly resonant low tones; they can be problematic. You're looking for depth without muddiness, with an even, low mid-range. Flatwound strings will produce warmer, thuddy sounds, whilst roundwound offer an edgy, twangier tone. Is the bass played near the bridge, or near the neck? This makes a significant difference, as does whether the player uses a pick or fingers. It's a personal preference, which affects the sound and feel in a big way. Fingers make plucked upstrokes that have plummier, rounder tones, whereas using a pick is more percussive when downstrokes are used, but can be loose and indistinct on upstrokes. Sometimes the click of the pick is an asset, but usually not. A little coaching on technique in pre-production never goes amiss.

Bass guitar is often effective simply DI'd into the recorder, but is arguably a little too close for comfort, so run a mic at the same time if you intend to do this. Even a small amount of miced signal mixed in with the DI has a more natural effect. Assign a track to each and balance as appropriate when mixing.

BASS GUITAR RECORDING TIPS
Bassists gravitate towards playing repeated riffs based on chord sequences. It's an easy way

out and shows they haven't lost any sleep over their part. But bass parts don't have to consist solely of root notes and triads (this is especially relevant to sequenced bass parts, where repetition rather than variety is the norm). It is better to think rhythmically about where to place notes most effectively – which is easily done by subtracting from predictable riff lines, with a little consideration of rhythm, harmony and counterpoint. The simplest exercise in rhythmic economy is limiting the number of bass notes to the beats of the kick-drum pattern.

The notes left out are just as important as those left in, but this is definitely easier said than done. Outstanding bass players have a natural feeling for negative space. Well-chosen notes and placement add an unexpected richness, colour and depth to the simplest of arrangements. Sir Paul is the undoubted master of that economic, melodic style; partly because of his sheer musicality and partly because the humble violin bass is difficult to negotiate and has inbuilt intonation problems. Basically, when you have a Hofner bass, avoid all the notes that sound like a washing machine. On the plus side, they sound fantastic if you can figure out how to record them properly.

Stand-Up Bass
Stand-up bass players tend to have a more economic style than electric bassists. The size of the instrument isn't quite as easy to navigate, Place a large dynamic or condenser mic 5–10cm (2–4in) away, between and facing towards the bridge and f-hole, and down a bit.

ELECTRIC GUITARS

Use a dynamic or condenser mic. For a dry, rock sound, place it 5cm (2in) away from the speaker, positioned 5–7cm (2–2.75in) from the centre of the cone. For a natural, open sound, move the mic back 10cm–1.25m (4in–4ft), depending on guitar and amplifier used, the throw of the speaker and the room. You need clarity, detail and enough mid-

The perennial 57 on the cone.

An alternate Neumann mic placed at a more discreet distance to capture the 'throw' of a Fender twin.

range so that it won't sound thin, but not so much that it loses definition. Some people like to use two or more mics, which usually means they end up somewhere in-between a good and poor result; mediocre, which is not a place you ever want to be. The settings on the amplifier and guitar are as crucial as the mic, as they can be all too easily brittle or muddy, or with unflattering distortion that is ineffectual in the mix. If the guitarist is using a pedal board, nine out of ten times it will be better without it. Electric guitars are loud and any loud instrument is deceptive. Check the sound through your monitors at a modest volume to hear what it's *really* like.

ELECTRIC GUITAR RECORDING TIPS

Whilst recording an electric guitar is not that challenging – just stick a mic in front of the amplifier, more or less – eliciting a performance with tones that work can well be.

Rhythm guitars need to be strong. Many players are handy with licks and solos, but far fewer are adept with rhythm. When the rhythm guitar sounds weak or flabby, it's usually the way it's being played. Try changing a loose up/down rhythm stroke to one using only downstrokes, which are more muscular and strident. Or possibly the playing is lazy because there is too much distortion, or stomp-box effects are overused. Often, a clearer, more middling tone will have more backbone and will cut through a mix better – but needs to be played well.

Lead guitarists may want to take you into 'The Land of a Million Overdubs'. I agree, it is difficult for a player to think through and organise overdubs prior to recording, but guitar parts should be carefully considered and condensed into a maximum of three, with distinct tonal changes. It is not true that layer upon layer of guitars will sound bigger.

Don't underestimate the use of tone for expansiveness and dynamics. Many guitarists have a favourite sound which they use on everything, or just switch by default from one pick-up to another, but overdubbing identical tones makes mush. The parts will fight for space and sound smaller than they should. Vary the tone, even slightly, and you'll notice more definition immediately. Much of Jimmy Page's work with Led Zeppelin consists of no more than two, at most three, electric guitar parts, using clever changes of tone to create panoramic dynamics. It's hard to believe, but listen carefully and you'll see. You don't need a lot if you have a good player, good parts and good tones.

Licks and solos played exclusively above the twelfth fret are boring at best, irritating at worst. We've heard it all before. Look for contrast between high and low notes, of sustained notes and clusters, with defined melody and phrasing. A player cramming in as many notes from a blues scale as possible in the allotted space to show what a virtuoso they are has the opposite effect – as all guitar-hero ego-tripping does. It's the appropriate, tasteful players that listeners rate as most accomplished.

Overdone distortion sounds like a cheap plastic hairdryer. The richest, most dimensional distortion is still an old-school guitar/valve-amp combination with a well-played, careful choice of guitar tones. Stomp boxes and amp 'overdrive' effects lend more clarity and impact in most cases if turned down a bit, but remain rather unconvincing and flat sounding for the most part. For a *truly* authentic Hairdryer vs Dentist Drill sonic, put your teeth and curlers in and DI the guitar through an old cassette deck with the recording levels completely maxed out.

ACOUSTIC GUITARS

A combination of two condenser mics, or either one, will work well on both steel- or nylon-strung acoustic guitars.

- **Microphone one** 10–15cm (4–6in) away from the twelfth fret, angled towards the sound-hole, or 5cm (2in) away for a more percussive effect.

Twelfth-fret mic gives definition, with the mic behind the bridge for body and resonance.

- **Microphone two** 5cm (2in) below and behind the bridge, 10cm (4in) away from the body, angled slightly towards the soundhole.

ACOUSTIC GUITAR RECORDING TIPS

Acoustics do sound good with a new set of strings, but these are guaranteed to go out of tune constantly if fitted the day before a session! An even rhythm technique will be needed from the acoustic player, or they'll sound weak, boomy or edgy. If this is the case, hitting the strings a little softer can help an acoustic basher, as can standing up while playing rather than sitting. If you're double tracking a rhythm part for texture, it's fine to match the sounds identically on both parts, but watch out for timing anomalies between them.

Aim for some light and shade in finger style or picked acoustic parts. Players are often worried about fret noise, fingerboard squeaks, creaks and whatnot. These are invariably best left in, as they add a lot to the feel. But keep an ear out for inadvertent foot tapping, or jacket or shirt cuffs rattling across the body of the guitar – they don't help at all.

KEYBOARDS

In general, other than acoustic pianos and perhaps old Hammond or vox organs, most keyboards will be recorded direct, without the need for a microphone. But you can still connect electronic keyboards via an amplifier and use the character of the room to make them feel more authentic. Use a condenser mic 15–60cm (6in–2ft) from the speaker, positioned just off the centre of the cone. In the event anyone has an old Rotating Leslie Cabinet, you'll need two mics, equally spaced, roughly 1.25m (4ft) apart, 60–80cm (2–2.6ft) away from the speaker.

KEYBOARD RECORDING TIPS

Like guitarists, keyboard players are not renowned for their economy and parts might need some serious weeding out in pre-production. Keyboard arrangements become cluttered by layering up too many indistinct parts, where simpler ones would cut through a mix more effectively. A single-note keyboard following the melody line of a song can add fullness tucked under a light vocal, underscore a focal point, or hammer home a hook line, as can a part in harmony with the vocal.

Big wodges of octave-spread chords are not usually dynamic – they will disappear in a mix rather than make a point. Ask a trained player – who will usually use octave-spread fingers – to play without pressing the highest key of the right hand and lowest key of the left. Shortening the width of the chords will clean up the part somewhat. For swirly/washy/pad organ parts, or orchestral string presets, try playing with one hand only, so as to sit more dynamically in the mix.

PIANOS

GRAND PIANO

Use two condenser microphones, roughly 15cm (6in) behind and 25–30.5cm (10–12in) above the hammers; one over the middle of the octave above Middle C, the other mic likewise, over the

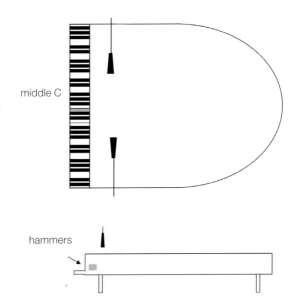

Grand piano set-up.

octave below Middle C. Even a single mic placed in the same way over Middle C can work very well.

Much depends on the piano itself – whether it's a baby grand, or a grand – and the size and shape of the room it sits in. Try adding a distant third mic if you want to pick up the sound of the room, but be discerning.

Upright Piano

Take the upper front panel off the piano, so that the hammers are exposed. You can leave the lid on, or take it off; whatever sounds best.

There are a lot of permutations in micing an upright; from the top or bottom of the case, one mic close, another distant. Every piano is different, so you should keep an open mind and experiment a little. I've been known to leave the front panel on, dangle a single, cheap dynamic mic inside and close the lid – which sounded great overloaded on tape, but wouldn't be advisable for a digital format!

- **(a) One microphone** Place a condenser or dynamic mic 7–10cm (2.75–4in) away from strings at Middle C, at a height halfway between the hammers and the top of the frame.
- **(b) Two microphones** As (a), but with two mics; one over octave above Middle C, the other an octave below it.

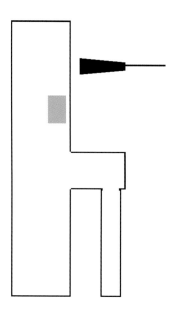

Upright piano, one microphone.

Piano Recording Tips

Trained pianists typically play lower octave notes with their left hand and melodic lines on upper octaves with their right. In the context of song material, the lower octaves may lack definition, whilst the upper octaves may sound fragmented and disconnected; a classical playing style doesn't compete terribly well with drums, bass and electric guitars. Simplifying the left-hand part to single notes instead of an octave spacing, and playing

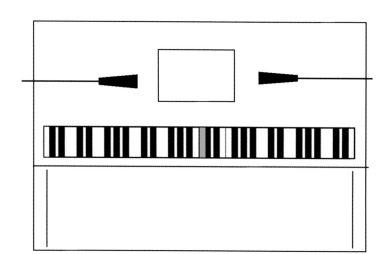

Upright piano, two microphones.

the right-hand part an octave lower, will give more shape and solidity, as can amending the right hand to playing rhythmic chords, with only single notes in featured spots. A piano part with this simple, mid-range rhythmic approach will add a lot of body to a track, as well as offering support for a rhythm guitar – sometimes even replacing it.

PERCUSSION

A condenser mic, 75cm–1.25m (2.5–4ft) from the source, will always work. It largely depends how loud the percussion instrument is. For some instruments, you may find a dynamic mic roughly 20cm (8in) away is more suitable. Some percussion instruments make loud, fast transients that will peak out at alarmingly low levels, so check your meters frequently!

For some unexplained reason, musicians flee from percussion overdubs, possibly because although they appear simple, the timing has to be spot-on accurate. Expect a look of panic next time someone suggests a tambourine part. All eyes will be on you!

STRINGS, ENSEMBLES AND ORCHESTRAS

You'll see from the diagrams that a pair of cardioid condenser microphones can be used in a variety of ways to record small to large ensembles and even orchestras. Which works best for you will depend on your mics, the size of the ensemble and the room they are in. I'd suggest starting with a spaced pair, angled slightly away from each other. A spaced pair need only have a distance of 15–20cm (6–8in) between them, or can be equidistant by as much as 1–1.25m (3–4ft); it's a very flexible configuration for ensemble applications.

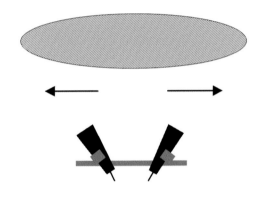

Small ensemble set-up using stereo bar.

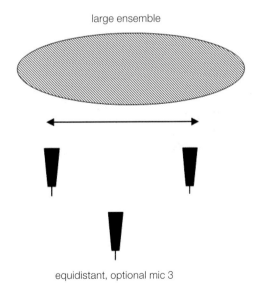

large ensemble

equidistant, optional mic 3

Experiment with the height of mics when recording large ensembles in big rooms, as the acoustics play a greater role in the end result; positioning them as high as your mic stands allow, pointing slightly downwards, can be very effective.

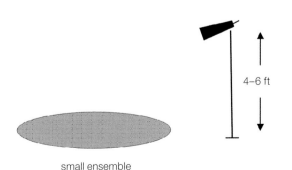

4–6 ft

small ensemble

One mic set-up for small ensembles.

Strings are generally used in ensembles. For soloists (typically violin or cello), a condenser mic 20–30cm (8–12in) away from the soundhole will usually suffice.

It is uncomfortable to wear headphones whilst playing orchestral instruments, so when using classically trained players for overdubs, give them time to adjust.

BRASS INSTRUMENTS
Brass instruments are loud. Use a large diaphragm condenser microphone that can withstand high SPLs, or a dynamic microphone, placed 10–20cm (4–8in) away from, and angled towards, the horn. Brass sections have a natural volume balance between them; a closely spaced pair at a distance of 60cm–1m (2–3ft) away works nicely.

WOODWIND INSTRUMENTS
A condenser mic will do the job, in a 10–20cm (4–8in) position away from the sound source. For flute or piccolo, I've also found that a Shure SM58 dynamic mic produces a solid representation, without predominant high frequencies.

EVERYTHING ELSE
At this juncture I'm tempted to say – for anything else, take the microphone of your choice, try it

10–20cm (4–8in) away, or a bit farther if it's very loud, and do as your ears tell you to see what works.

VOCALS

The vast majority of vocals are recorded with condenser mics, as they capture the most sensitivity and detail. Large diaphragm condensers are generally preferred. But dynamics can be more than adequate and sometimes a better choice for male rock vocals. For a rich, warm sound, ribbon microphones are very attractive, but don't tolerate loud volumes or peaks well.

The vocalist should stand 15–30.5cm (6–12in) away from a condenser mic and at about 10–15cm (4–6in) away if a dynamic is your choice. It depends how loud their voice is. The airspace changes tone, detail and level. Too close will create plosives and sibilance, which are troublesome to fix, and the resulting proximity effect (especially with dynamic microphones) will bulge the low frequencies. A pop shield will contain some of this, but not necessarily all.

What you need more than anything is a good performance. Without that, you're sunk. You may be able to improve a poor performance to some extent, but you can never fix it, regardless of any technology you have. A great performance will stand any amount of mistreatment, or deficiencies in the recording.

PREPARATION
Make sure that you have good communication with the vocalist through the talkback and a direct line of sight for cueing and direction. Singing lead vocals to a control room full of people on the other side of the glass can be a vulnerable and intimidating experience, so limit band members, friends, family pets and hangers on to an absolute

Just one more for level.

minimum. It's lonely in the spotlight. If a vocalist is very nervous, or performs better in privacy, screen them off, turn the lights down and do whatever will best provide comfort and reassurance. Now and then, it can be better to record vocals in the control room with you – or even sitting next to them in the recording area itself. A vocalist needing lots of support and encouragement will benefit from close contact. But you will both need to wear headphones!

Provide the best monitoring possible. Pay attention to requests for less/more track, louder/quieter volume. It will save lots of time. But discourage pleadings for reverb; it has a bad effect on accurate pitching. Suggest that the vocalist either pushes one side of the headphones behind one ear, or holds them very slightly away from the ears (watch out for feedback). It minimises pitch problems and tames overenthusiastic delivery.

Mic Technique for the Vocalist

It helps immensely when a vocalist knows where and when they sing louder or quieter than the norm. Every vocalist has to work hard to reach certain notes, which can push the levels so much that they peak out and distort. And bear in mind that a vocalist will always sing louder when they settle in, so allow enough headroom for that. The best way to get an even level is for the vocalist to lean back a little, away from the mic (or turn the head slightly to one side) to compensate for loud notes, controlling their own level in an intuitive, natural way by moving away from the microphone like this. And vice versa for the quietest spots. It's a subtle technique and requires a practised vocalist to work seamlessly, but is always much better than adding heavy compression, or madly riding faders during the mix. It also helps the feel of a vocal.

Coach the inexperienced, even in a basic way, and you'll hear a dramatic improvement. There are bound to be some loud and quiet places; you should expect that. Mark cues on a lyric sheet as you need to, so that it's easy to find and adjust when you mix.

Sonics

The choice of mic and quality of performance will outweigh any amount of EQ or other effects that you could ever think of. Evaluate at what volume level the vocalist produces the best tone. Most push too hard and will be pleasantly surprised how much better it sounds when they sing just a tad quieter. Let them hear a test! Bumps are evened out, tone is more consistent and they have more control. I have rarely asked a vocalist to sing louder.

Sibilance

Sibilance occurs when 'essss' sounds become louder than they should be. See if changing the mic distance, singing slightly across the mic, or using a pop shield solves it. If the problem persists, move the mic and point it at the singer's nose, but ask them to sing to the front, where the mic was. It did take me a week to adjust manually an album's worth of the sibilant 'esses' from a Spanish vocalist …

Plosives

Sudden Ps, Bs and other hard syllables can create pops, bulges and level clipping. Good microphone technique is the best remedy, or a pop shield. Mesh pop shields affect the tone less than foam ones. But if you're in a tight corner and desperate, stuffing a sock in the vocalist's mouth will have to suffice.

Extraneous Noise

Ask the vocalist before recording begins not to tap their feet, rustle lyric sheets, touch the mic, or indulge in performance pyrotechnics. If they simply *have* to jump around, give 'em a Shure 57 and hope for the best. Expect to remind them about the foot tapping later.

Before you Begin

Estimate two to three hours to record a lead vocal with a less than experienced vocalist. It's far better to overestimate than end up with a hurried, second-rate performance. Vocalists generally underestimate how long they will need. Very few can deliver a keeper in a full take, so anticipate alternates and plenty of punch-ins. Assign one track for the lead vocal and another for alternates and repairs. Keep a third track free and once you've successfully completed recording the vocal and any repairs, ask them to do another complete take from start to finish on this spare track. Sometimes vocalists really loosen up, knowing that they have a decent vocal safely in the can and will give you a take that eclipses the previous ones. Record all warm-ups and rehearsals for the same reason. I recommend recording a 'run through for level' without their knowledge. Sometimes you get lucky.

RECORDING STRATEGY

Using a complete copy of the lyric sheet, make notes of keeper parts and repairs as you record. Always go for complete takes before doing repairs. A 'let's do the choruses first' mentality, which some folk advocate, completely destroys feel and undermines the vocalists' confidence.

As a rule, expect the first couple of takes to be tentative, especially the first verse and chorus, though you may get some good lines here and there. By the end of take two, the vocalist is settling in and will likely do well on take three:

1. Run through 'for level' – a complete take. Record it without the vocalist's knowledge.
2. Take one: a complete take, without interruption, whether good or bad.
3. Take two: a complete take, without interruption, if take one is below par.
4. Take three: a complete take, on your secondary track.

The vocalist may want to hear what they've done, but ask them to wait until the repairs have been addressed.

Now you'll need to assess what you have that's workable and what repairs are needed. It will more than likely already be clear to you which take is best, so focus on that one. Your cue sheet should tell you where to locate the first repair.

Punch-Ins

It's always more natural to replace a whole line or phrase, rather than a word or two. Give the vocalist enough pre-roll and ask them to sing along with the track before and after the cue. It really helps in replicating the feel of the part they're replacing. Listen for consistency of level and tone, ensuring that the vocalist maintains the same distance from the mic, so that the repairs will match up and be invisible. You'll need to check the punch, so let the vocalist know when you're doing that – 'checking!' – or they may well sing again, thinking it's a retake.

You may prefer to work through the repairs from start to finish, but depending on the performance level of the vocalist and the complexity of the song, it's sometimes better to focus on the identical sections first, before moving on to potentially more difficult places:

5. Repairs – choruses.
6. Repairs – verses.
7. Repairs – any weak entry lines or particularly difficult spots.

It is the repairs that will eat all the time and the vocalist – and yourself – will feel the pressure is off once they are complete and that is the time for Just One More:

8. Take four – a final complete 'feel' take on your third track, once repairs have been completed.

You might find that you have keeper parts on two or more vocal takes. If the cue points are clear and levels match, you can edit or bounce them together on one track now, while it's freshest in your mind, or do it ahead of mixing. Don't wait until your mix is ready to add the vocals.

Fixing Problems

Listen carefully not just to pitch, feel and timing, but for overall consistency in level and tone. Pay close attention to the first word in each line. It's not uncommon for the end of the first syllable to disappear if it is sung slightly off the beat. 'And', 'but', ''cause' are typical examples of this and will end up sounding like a grunt if you're not careful. Likewise, the ends of lines and words may disappear, where a loud, hard consonant is followed by a soft syllable. Some fader moves or level editing will rectify this, but good mic technique is preferred.

Many vocalists have bad habits they're unaware of. The most popular is late entry, by half a beat, to the first line of a verse or chorus. It makes the verse or chorus weak and is a liability. The second commonplace mannerism is an overly dramatic, self-conscious feel. Discourage any pre-planned 'improvisation' – 'Yeah!', 'Woo!', 'Well, I'll go to our house' and the like – and ask them to sing in a simpler, more direct way, without vocal gymnastics. Singing more quietly is very effective in undermining an overachiever.

Self-consciousness is sometimes manifested in perfectionism, where a vocalist is obsessive about insignificant details. Reassure them that you're keenly aware of the parts in question and can be trusted to deal with them properly. Then distract them by directing their attention to the song as a whole.

Double Tracking
Double tracking works because of the slight varia-tions when a vocalist sings exactly the same part on two different tracks. The performance has to be almost, but not quite, identical. This method is very handy for strengthening a weaker vocalist, adding warmth, or lifting the dynamics of a chorus. It has a characteristic of its own that can be useful in the arrangement, emphasising a chorus or other focal point. Real double tracking is far superior to any 'doubler' software.

HARMONY AND BACKING VOCALS
First and foremost, the vocal parts must be worked out correctly. Check them for accuracy in the control room, where communication is easy, and rehearse any changes the parts may need. Focus on pitching and phrasing. Set up the monitoring so that the lead vocal is as loud or quiet as the vocalist needs in order to pitch against it, or intonation will be difficult. The 'one headphone off' ploy works especially well here.

MULTIPLE VOCALS
If there are two vocalists to be recorded together (for backing vocals, perhaps), place them each at 45 degrees to the front of and 30–60cm (1–2ft) away from a cardioid pattern mic and balance the blend by having the louder of the two back away from the microphone a little. For three vocalists at the same time, you'll have one in the centre, and another on each side, grouped around the mic.

4

TRACKING

I asked a colleague of mine recently if he'd had any difficulties tracking a new band. 'Getting them to sound good,' he replied.

2-TRACK

When you think about multitrack recording, it's easy to forget that stereo is, in fact, 2- track, if each channel is treated independently. You could say that many UK early 1960s 'stereo' records – the ones with all the instruments on one side and vocals on the other – were really 2-track, not stereo. What's the difference? When you use a 2-track method to record, it's with the intention that it will be mixed afterwards, using each track to group and balance the instruments in a specifically different way from each other, and no more so than when you only have two microphones to work with.

You can record in 2-track on any handheld recorder, or even a cassette deck, as long as you can attach two separate, independent microphones to it. You don't need a mixer. What's the use of that, you might ask? Plenty, especially if you don't have a mixer to make fader cues with at the time. You will still have some leeway to rebalance and cue instruments when mixing and minimise the glitches that frequently occur in live performances, in a way that would not be possible with a straight stereo recording. I've made several 2-track albums, on location at live shows, or in rooms used as dedicated recording spaces, with nothing but a recorder and two mics. (Perhaps the strangest was in an old oyster cannery with a long concrete table running the entire length. No seafood was harmed.)

The simplest method of making a 2-track recording employs a pair of mics, each assigned to its own track. The aim is not to create a stereo balance between them, but to record two individually balanced mono tracks. At its simplest, you might have instruments on track one and vocals on track two. Or you could balance two groups of instruments in a mono or fake stereo mix. One track may be predominantly drums and bass, the other a balance of vocals and guitars. The two separate tracks are treated individually in the mix, with any necessary level cues and effects, then balanced together as desired. With good placement and the correct panning, you can even cue solos, fills and other parts that need more focus, or less volume.

You would expect some spillage between the mics, but a little bleed is a good thing for the integrity of a performance; 2-track can work especially well for groups of acoustic instruments and small ensembles.

STEREO

Take one of your two microphones – cardioid condensers are the best choice – and using the 'close your eyes and point technique', try to find the 'sweet spot', where the sound is most balanced and attractive. It's likely to be at, or near, to the central point of where the performers are positioned. Mark the spot with a mic stand, or a piece of tape.

If you are using a stereo bar (a flat piece of metal or plastic, with two moveable mic clips attached to it), set your mics, angled away from each other by

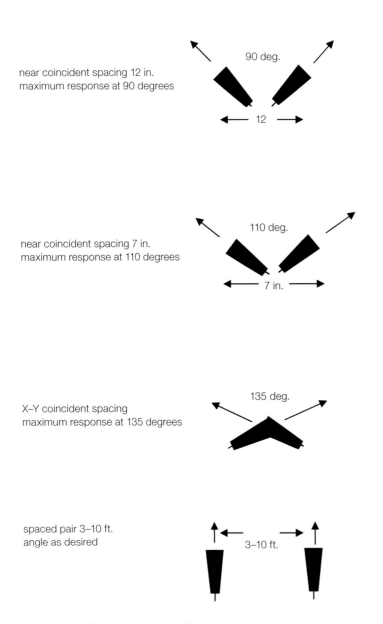

near coincident spacing 12 in.
maximum response at 90 degrees

90 deg.

← 12 →

near coincident spacing 7 in.
maximum response at 110 degrees

110 deg.

← 7 in. →

X–Y coincident spacing
maximum response at 135 degrees

135 deg.

spaced pair 3–10 ft.
angle as desired

3–10 ft.

Some stereo configurations for cardioid microphones.

When recording a large group of musicians, orchestras, big bands, or choirs, the mics should be placed in front of the musicians, most likely 2m (6.5ft)+ high, angled downward and away from each other, 60cm (2ft) or more apart.

If your system only allows you to record a limited number of tracks at the same time, you can balance the relative levels and cues for multiple mics using an external analogue mixer and send them to the stereo input of your recording interface. Back in the Stone Age, when only a small number of tracks were available, grouping channels together (subgroups) was done as a matter of course. It's not an approach everyone would prefer, as the balance from the mixer can't be changed later. But that's not a bad lesson to learn.

SEPARATION AND BLEED

When recording a typical band playing together, there will be spillage between some, if not all, of the instruments. No-noise fanatics would put each of them in isolation booths, which is a terrible way for a band to work. They're used to the sound they make together as a unit and it's never the same if everyone is in different rooms wearing headphones, no matter how long you spend adjusting their monitoring balance. Iso booths are an antiseptic 1970s hangover as far as I'm concerned; they were never a good idea, despite the reasoning behind them.

about 22–30cm (9–12in), where the stereo image is most coherent. Or if you don't have a stereo bar, position the mics 15cm (6in) away from each other, equidistant from 'X marks the spot', then angle them away from each other roughly 5–7cm (2–2.75in), until the stereo image comes into focus.

There are simpler ways to contain the bleed among instruments that will give enough separation without hindering the musicians, or the integrity of the recording – good old baffles. They're effective and less intrusive than booths or screens, although I would consider screens with a window in them if a vocalist is singing live with the track.

The other option is where to place the amplifiers; you don't want the bass amp directly facing a guitar amplifier, for example. Let the musicians set themselves up as they wish. You can always move, or angle amplifiers away from each other to suit.

GROUPS OF MUSICIANS

One of the main things, if you're recording a band, or any group of musicians, is to keep everyone focused on the job in hand. Musicians are easily distracted when setting up, in particular. It does take a drummer longer to set up than anyone else. By the time they're finished, the others can have gone off the boil, especially if Mr Drummer says he needs another ten minutes for a cuppa or fag break before he's in the mood. Whenever possible, I'll book a couple of extra hours of studio time the evening before a session purely for setting up, so that everyone is fresh the next day and we can get rolling without any undue delays. There are times when you just have to roll with it, of course; like the charming French band who turned up with a trolley full of groceries to get their lunch cooking before they were prepared to start, or an Argentinian band that stopped off to *buy their instruments* on their way from the airport to the studio.

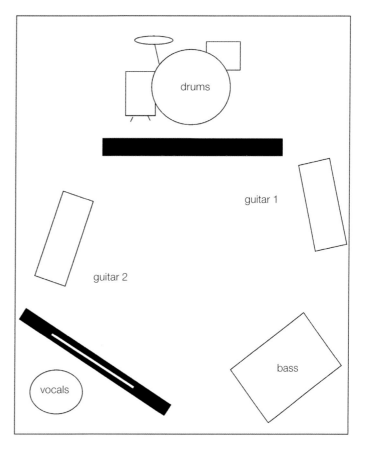

How to set up baffles.

But these are exceptions and both bands were wonderful.

If you can't arrange to set up the instruments and mics the evening prior to the session, allow two to three hours for it and work as fast as you can. You don't want the band to get restless or lose their edge waiting around with nothing to do during a long set-up period. If boredom sets in, it's difficult to get a disciplined, positive performance.

Recording, by and large, feels unnatural for musicians; they're in a windowless room with no audience and are nervous under the microscope of recording. Headphones are uncomfortable and intimidating, and anyone overdubbing on their own is bound to feel exposed and vulnerable to some extent, so do your best to make them feel secure and confident. I like to let a band set up in the way that's most familiar to them, often, as they might do in rehearsal. They need to be comfortable, with a good line of sight and where they can all hear each other as much as possible. Then they don't have to wear headphones at all; I just set up a speaker for talkback and let them play as normal. No one is in an isolation booth and baffles are only used if absolutely necessary – in front of the drums or bass perhaps, or if the vocalist is singing live. I've found it much easier to get good performances that way, with a natural interplay of the instruments.

Each player needs to hear themself in context with the other musicians in the way that they are accustomed. So why wear headphones if you don't have to? They physically get in the way and at best only approximate an artificial representation of the sound. Give a vocalist headphones, certainly, or they won't be able to hear – but only over one ear. That will help with pitching, while keeping them connected with the band. It's unlikely you'll record a keeper live vocal performance when recording basic tracks, but you should try anyway. If the vocalist also plays an instrument, they should sing and play at the same time. It adds to the overall feel and dynamic quite significantly. When headphones are a must, give all band members the same sound balance. Otherwise, you'll spend an hour or more customising mixes for each individual, which really will make no difference at all.

Keeping a convivial atmosphere in the studio eases nerves and helps everyone. But maintain momentum and be disciplined enough to work to your schedule. Note which musician is the leader and use them to keep the band on the ball. Offer your reassurance to the weakest player; tell them they're doing well.

Double-check the arrangements and tempo. Bands play faster under pressure without realising it and sometimes an 'inspired' member will change his part the night before. And do try to get an audible count in.

Record all the musicians at once. It doesn't make any sense to me that the basic tracks should only consist of drums, or drums and bass, and that all other parts are best overdubbed later. Not only is this a misguided idea, it puts pressure on the rhythm section to overperform, whilst encouraging sloppiness in their bandmates. A band is the sum of all its parts and to dismantle that at the first stage of recording is a mistake. You don't record an orchestra in separate parts.

Before you start recording, tell the band not to put down their instruments, move from their positions, chat at the end of a take, or stop playing until you say so. What may sound like an error to a player at the time may well be a great, unexpected 'feel' moment. Tell them to expect to record a second take right after the first is complete, so that they keep on their toes. Quite often a band will settle in nicely during the last third of a performance and doing another take immediately, while they're still 'on it', will pay dividends. So stay in record mode.

Keep drink swigging between takes to a minimum. When one musician reaches for his bottle, the others will inevitably follow, and it will break the concentration of them all. Give them a breather after three or four takes and don't allow a lunch break before you have the basic track recorded, or you'll lose an hour afterwards before they're fully engaged again. You can get the best out of a group's performance curve as follows:

1. Do a run-through (record this without the band's knowledge).
2. Take one – likely to settle in midway through. Record take two immediately after.
3. Take two – let the band have a few seconds after the take is complete for water, chatter, but don't let them put down their instruments.
4. Take three – if this is better than take two, record take four immediately afterwards. If not, stop at the first significant error and retake.
5. If you have a workable take by now, tell the band they've got it and ask them to record a final one, just for fun. Occasionally, they'll relax

just a little bit more and deliver a fine performance, though more often than not it will be a sloppy take with everyone bashing it out.

Next, check the best take yourself, especially for timing errors, but don't let the band listen yet. They'll overanalyse their performances and it's more important to finish any remaining tracking first. If they didn't nail the first song in four takes, move on to the next and come back to it later.

After tracking is complete, take a break and let the band hear playbacks. You'll already know which are the best takes, but they'll need to listen for their own benefit.

SOLO ARTISTS

Working with solo artists is much the same as working with a band, but the relationship is solely between you and the artist, so closer because of it. There are no other band members to look to for support, therefore it's important that you can be considered a trusted ally who can be relied upon to fix any problems. You've probably gone some way towards establishing this during pre-production, and recording puts more focus on it; the artist on one side of the glass and you on the other. It might well feel that there is more responsibility on your shoulders. Take the same approach in the recording process with a solo artist as you would a band. Remember, it's more daunting out there for a solo musician, so foster a caring, intimate atmosphere and offer sincere support frequently.

OVERDUBS

Efficiency, pace and patience are needed, or overdub sessions will turn into a long slog. Group overdubs by type in order to minimise set-up time and focus the players – all electric guitars, then all acoustic guitars, all keyboards and so on. If you have skilled musicians, you may be able to record two or more of them at once, as long as their parts are well rehearsed, thereby keeping a unified feel to the entire recording. Harmony vocals will work especially well when recorded in groups, though it is demanding on the vocalists.

Decide whether overdubs will be done in the studio, with headphones, or in the control room. It's often more relaxed in the control room and makes for easier communication, especially when refining parts. When headphones are needed, spend enough time giving the musicians an optimum monitoring balance.

CUE SHEETS

Always have a cue sheet for tracking performances, whether it's a full band, overdubs or vocals. Use a full lyric sheet for this, which should include any and all repeated sections, such as choruses, so that you're able to make notes line by line. You can add 'intro', 'solo', 'coda', or other reference points in the spaces where they happen. It's easier to follow and less distracting than watching a time display and will give you a more accurate impression of the performances.

Have a couple of coloured pens or pencils on hand, each designated for a different take. It's especially useful for comparing live takes and vocals (which may be compiled or A/B'd for the mix). As a take is performed, follow the cue sheet closely as you listen and note any questionable places as they happen by underlining the words. In the case of live-band tracking, you may find longer sections needing attention.

Your notes will give you a clear picture, at a glance, of the strength of each performance and where you may need to repair, edit, or retake parts. If you don't have a satisfactory take after three attempts, pause briefly and focus on the problem areas before trying another. Alternatively, move on to something else and revisit later. It's important to keep a session moving and not to

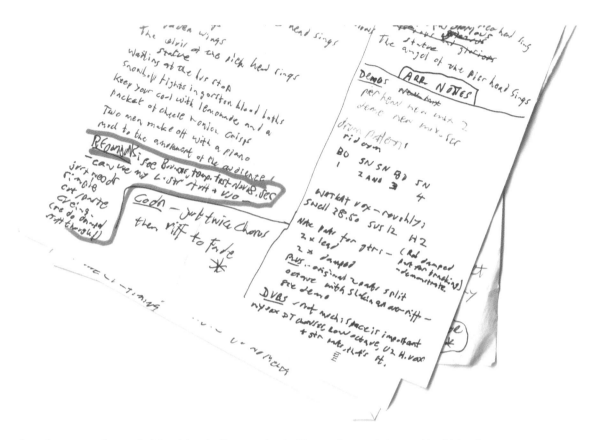

One of my own, rather undisciplined, handwritten cue sheets. No one else needed to read it, did they?

be sidetracked by errors for too long. The great thing about recording is that you can always do it again.

PERFORMANCE CURVE

You need to anticipate when musicians are about to reach their performance peak and guide them towards it by the pace you set. Start in a relaxed manner, then work faster as the performance improves. The aim is to capture as much as you can while the musicians are at their best, so be swift at locating record/rewind and punch-in points, minimise comments to single, encouraging words and push the momentum forwards.

Often, peak performances are fifteen to twenty minutes into a take, lasting for around ten minutes;

longer for someone who's used to recording. Hopefully, you will get most of what you need in that period. Check what you have, then let the performer hear what they did. But don't let them take off the headphones, or move from their spot, as this breaks the flow and it will take time to get the feel back again.

Work through your cue sheet, making repairs one at a time. It can be productive to start with chorus punch-ins, as they're repetitive and less challenging as a rule. Don't worry if the first line of a verse or chorus is poor. Entry points can be difficult, so it's more efficient to complete all the repairs, then go back and grab an errant line or two.

PERFORMANCE PSYCHOLOGY

When you're recording someone, you need to instil confidence in them (and in yourself), so that

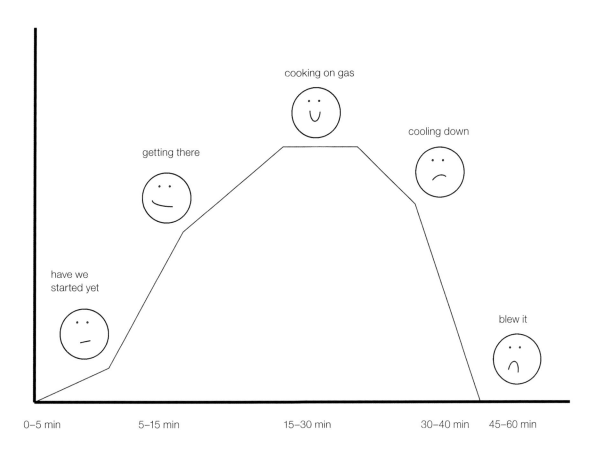

cooking on gas

cooling down

getting there

have we
started yet

blew it

| 0–5 min | 5–15 min | 15–30 min | 30–40 min | 45–60 min |

The performance curve.

they perform to the best of their ability. Let them know that they have the talent and skill to produce a brilliant performance – even if you know it might be a struggle. Help them to trust you enough to take your word for it when you say a take is fine, or that another is needed.

During recording, you'll need to use all your interpersonal skills to motivate, encourage, or constructively criticise. Patience is a virtue, as is diplomacy. By and large, just Be Nice and don't tell them what to do – at least not in so many words. I've found it's okay to be quite blunt about timing and phrasing issues, which, curiously, are seldom taken personally. Odd, as timing errors always sound like mistakes, whereas being slightly out of tune on occasion, which is always a sore point, can be good for feel now and again.

If you have a weak performer, your talkback reply will be along the lines of 'one more for confidence', after assuring them that what you already have is absolutely fine – even if it's not. Good excuses for retakes if you've run into difficult, road-blocking repairs are 'another one for level', or 'bad punch-in – my fault'. It's worth throwing in one or two of those anyway, to show that you make errors too. I've gone so far as to make a sign with 'One More' written on it and held it up at the window at the end of a take, to lighten the mood when a band was getting stuck. Deliver criticism with a light touch. We artistic types need to be reassured that we're doing a good job and you care about us. Don't always hit rewind as soon as you hear a mistake; it sends a message you're frustrated with the progress.

You'll run into difficult spots where you've already tried a number of punch-ins/repairs without success. Usually, it will be a particular line, word, or phrase that has tough timing or pitch, which a bit of repetition will solve. Just remain calm and say 'well done' when the task is accomplished. If the punch-in is just not happening, switch to another section and return to the difficult spot later. If a performer is overly anxious, or a bit too precious about their baby, distract them from it by getting them to concentrate solely on you and your directions; pretty much hold their hand through the performance.

When you're unlucky enough to have a prima donna on your hands, give credit where it's due, but don't hesitate to tell them straight about where and why there are problems. Probably no one has told them the truth before and they will respect that and follow your direction. You hope.

MIDI AND ELECTRONIC SOUNDS/ SAMPLES AND SEQUENCING

Samples and sequencing have analogue roots. One of the most well-known and ingenious exponents was Delia Derbyshire, who worked at the BBC Radiophonic Workshop during the 1960s. In that era, there were no samples, sequencers or drum machines, just tape recorders, frequency filters, oscilloscopes and suchlike. You had to invent sounds.

Delia's most famous work was the theme to the *Doctor Who* television series. For this, she recorded herself twanging a rubber band, slowed down at different speeds to create what were, effectively, samples made from tape loops, manually sequenced into the clever, two-note bass line. The melody was made with a test-tone generator, by turning the frequency dial back and forth in real time – a primitive monophonic synthesiser. Everything was recorded live. Someone managed the tape loops – secured by holding them with a pencil as they ran through the tape machine – as Delia took care of the melody and mix cues.

It was remarkably inventive and sounds just as pioneering and unique now as it did then. The recording would have been impossible to do without working out the exact details first. The calculations for slowing down the tape speed percentages into specific notes, editing the loops together for the right pattern and length, how to design the sounds from the frequency filters, all had to be meticulously planned, created and rehearsed. All from imagining what a twanging rubber band would sound like if you slowed it down. And I've never heard of anyone else who could tell you what the instrumentation of a record was just by looking at the shapes of the groove in a vinyl disc. That's how good she was.

Of course, there are ready-made sampled sounds available of just about anything you can think of – apart from those you invent for yourself. Don't spend more time auditioning the sounds than actually using them! It's always best to have a firm idea of the sound you want, rather than searching for something inspiring. You'll always end up using the first one you tried. The best thing is to make your own, if you can.

If you use synthesisers and samples, you'll find that many of them are 'finished' sounds, very complete and perfect sounding, but unrealistically so (bass guitar comes to mind!). To humanise these sounds, you probably already have tried dequantising them, which helps to some degree. How about decompressing them too, to emulate a more realistic ebb and flow? Decompression is the opposite of compression and some software compressors have this feature. You have to proceed with caution and not overdo it. It's best used in a subtle way and is literally guesswork and just using your ears. Load up a very compressed mix and try a little decompression on it; you'll get an idea of how it can be a complete wreck if overdone, or helpful when the settings are sympathetic. Then you might try it on a sampled drum kit or other instruments. It's one of those things that when it helps, it helps a lot.

Sequenced, cut and paste generated tracks

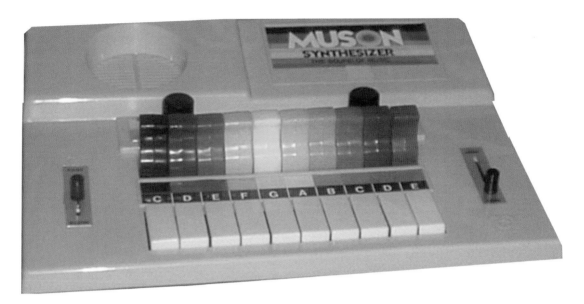

'Pegs in the hole' plastic synthesiser, based on the same principles as the VCS3.

don't require mics, or musicians, except for perhaps a vocal. In effect, every track is an overdub and more about assembling an effective musical arrangement than capturing a performance. Resist the temptation to create layers of repetitive sequences. If the parts are right, you don't need many. First and foremost, the strength of the material is crucial, no matter what the sounds consist of, or how they are shaped.

BE IMPERFECT

A canny auld Scotsman said to me as we were about to record – 'I want ye tae leave a' the mistakes in.' It was good advice.

How many times have you painted yourself into a corner, taking and retaking, EQ-ing, compressing, recompressing, or nudging the edit of a problem sound that *still* doesn't work for you?

Recording can sometimes feel like the cart is pulling the donkey. The reality is, you don't get it right some of the time and you have to live with it. But, more often than not, listening three weeks later to that awkward, embarrassing little bit you fudged on the mix is inaudible to everyone, including yourself, who will be paying more attention to it than anyone else on the planet. Errors – or perceived errors – are like that. You just need to know when to quit if things get out of proportion and what is really a mistake, or not.

As a rule of thumb, timing errors are the audible ones, so fix them. Nothing else will be noticeable, or considered a problem, unless it's REALLY obvious. And recognise that the human element of not actually being perfect is not a bad thing to have. This is why we always like the 'demo' better than the finished thing. It's in the moment, unselfconscious and we're not at all worried about the mistakes – it's a demo, isn't it?

CHANNEL ONE
Meter Trim

-30 -25 -20 -15 -10 -6 -4 -2 -1 0

GAIN REDUCTION (dB)

5
MIXING

LISTENING

I have had no formal training as a recording or mastering engineer, or as a producer. I learnt by listening and doing, watching people work, making lots of mistakes and gradually building a store of knowledge to draw upon. I could always imagine what the finished record should be in my head; the hard bit was figuring out how you made that happen.

One thing is always true; listening is the greatest asset. Living things respond to sound. It's essential, so that you can run away fast enough when that spider is after you, or hear where your family members are if you get lost.

Our inventive little human brains discovered that you could assemble sounds in all kinds of interesting ways to communicate more effectively and to evoke emotional responses in the listener through language and music. Everyone has a natural, instinctive ear and just about anyone can tell you if the vocal is too quiet on a record, or someone missed a beat. Except perhaps for the people involved in recording it, who are still preoccupied with whether + or −0.25dB would have made all the difference.

The weight of analytical and practical knowledge needed to make sound recordings effectively, and the preconceptions, 'how tos', 'dos and don'ts' and the 'should it be like this or nots', all get in the way of our innate responses. Sometimes you literally can't hear the wood for the trees, as it were. There is a tendency to overthink when the process has a very long list of instructions and conflicting information, as well as needing objective decision-making and some mechanical and technical aptitude. After all that, it's little wonder we sometimes don't know which end is up.

Hearing is easily confused and can be easily fooled; just ask yourself, when you've been EQing an empty channel by mistake for ten minutes before you realised what you were doing. In many ways making a record is, to some degree, about fooling your hearing, rather like a film tricks your brain into assembling the individual frames as a moving picture. Of course, we can slow down the projector and examine each image. But it only actually makes any real sense when the film is played back at the right speed. I bet film editors have the same problem we do.

Context is everything. An isolated sound – no matter how much it is bent and shaped and processed – is no more than a brush mark in a painting, or a single word on a page. Every sound is entirely dependent on the other sounds that surround it and the silence with which it exists. It seems obvious, but is something that's easily forgotten or misinterpreted when we're able to manipulate sound in an almost microscopic way. Mixing involves being able to listen to all the individual components in isolation, yet always as part of the whole, hundreds upon hundreds of times.

So how on earth can you be objective about your own work?

Most people listen to music passively, without undue attention to detail – with little or no preconceptions about it. In the 'Wonderful World of Recording', passive listening only truly happens on first hearing. Thereafter, active listening takes over, as we deliberately listen to the nuances of sound and arrangement, and wonder 'How did they do that?' It's through this active listening that we gradually train our ears to analyse individual sounds and what makes them tick. The more adept a listener you are, the easier it becomes to create musical arrangements, identify and improve the fine detail of sonics, assess performances and balance and mix recordings. It is a skill that develops over time and with experience. The more recordings you make, the better you 'hear'.

There's a certain detachment that comes with active listening, which can be hard to switch off. For example, you've been listening to the bass in isolation, but when you put it in the mix you can't decide whether it's too loud or too quiet in the context of everything else. That requires passive listening and switching between active and passive is not necessarily easy to do. That's why you hit a wall after working on something a little too long and can't tell if it's good or not anymore. Whenever you're up against this, the only real solution is to get away from it and come back a day or three later – or longer, sometimes. Overlistening will do that to you, so to avoid this you really do have to take frequent ear breaks, even if only for five minutes.

It's important to listen in context as well as in isolation, because everything in a recording affects everything else. That might sound crazy, but when you make an adjustment to part of a mix, it has a knock-on effect. Bring up the drums, you hear less of the vocal. Even small changes make a difference; a level change of 0.20dB is audible, or at least *feels* audible. So you can imagine what brickwall compression on a guitar is capable of.

To train yourself to hear actively and critically, go through the favourites from different eras in your music collection. Concentrate as intently as you can, without distractions, and try to identify all the different instruments and the roles they play. Examine how the parts relate to each other in tone, level and dynamics, melody, harmony and rhythm. Listen for the space between the notes, look at the focal points and transitions, and why they work. Surprisingly small changes in an arrangement or mix can have a lot of impact. Hear how mood and character is created and developed.

Taking a Test Drive

Here's a challenge; you can do this now, or when you're finished reading the book.

Open up a mix you've previously done and take off all the effects and any panning you used. Now make a new mix of the song using only level adjustments. Do your best, but don't spend any longer than three hours on it.

Once you're done, listen through it once and write down everything you think is wrong, as well as all the things you like about it. Be as honest and objective as you can. This will reveal some specific areas you need to think about. Maybe it was hard to balance due to the number of tracks used for punching in parts. Would it have been better to get a stronger performance instead of all those punch-ins? Perhaps the bass was muddy, or less punchy than you remembered it. Was that down to how it was recorded, or was your monitoring the culprit? Maybe vocals were masked by the keyboards, or cut through this mix quite nicely. Or you spotted something that wasn't working well in the arrangement. How would you fix it?

Now load up your original mix, listen again and take notes in the same way – what you liked, what you didn't. Go and get a cup of tea, then come back and compare the two sets of notes. What does that tell you?

Pay attention and try to pick them apart. But don't be concerned about trying to identify specific frequencies, or other technical stuff. It's more valuable to build up your knowledge of how different instruments occupy space in the sound spectrum. Developing your listening is similar to improving your sense of pitch when learning an instrument – the more you practise, the more accurate it becomes.

Mixing paints the sonic landscape. Like a painting, the composition as a whole conveys the message and the subtleties enrich it. It is the relationships between the sounds that create the characteristics, momentum, tension and release, light and shade. Learn how to listen to individual parts and cross-reference them as your mix progresses. Each affects the other and you'll need all the dispassionate objectivity you can muster. Work from broad brushstrokes to fine detail.

MONITORING THE MIX

You will already have checked the gain structure in your DAW when setting up your monitoring and noted the most accurate level to listen at in your room. This is the volume reference point that you will always go back to, regardless of the number of times you will need to listen louder and quieter during mixing.

Volume levels creep up as each new component is added. Compensate as you go by turning down the output level in your mixing window to avoid clipping and distortion. When you're isolating sounds to check or edit, you may want to monitor a little louder; once you're done, return the level to where it was to listen in context. As a mix progresses it can be useful to turn down the volume. This is good for spotting inconsistencies in the overall balance and EQ (as does checking in mono, if you can. I'm surprised my stereo/mono button hasn't worn out yet). The louder your monitoring volume, the faster you'll burn out, so take a short break the minute things stop making sense. It is also useful to cross-reference on a second set of monitors, if you have some.

HOW LONG?

It matters less how long something takes, than establishing a smooth workflow with momentum. Make quick decisions based on what you hear and take that short ear break each hour to keep a clear head. Inevitably, awkward things come up that misbehave. It's easy to get bogged down and wrestle with an uncooperative sound longer than you should. If you've tried a few options to no avail, leave it and move on to something else. Come back with fresh ears later and it will be much easier to figure out how to fix it.

Limit mixing sessions to a maximum of six hours per day or you'll burn out; concentrated, repetitive listening wears you down. It helps a lot to break down the process into convenient, logical increments – rough balance, level adjustments, fader cues, effects, final balance – and take a decent breather after each. Some things are more taxing and time-consuming than others, so resting your ears will be necessary to keep your perspective as the mix develops.

Though you should never neglect essentials like vocal placement, or dealing with messy cues, you can overwork and mix the life out of a track if you spend too long on it. Don't become sidetracked by secondary detail. It's easy to forget the big picture and become obsessive about small, irritating things that bug you when you're getting tired (sibilance is a good one). So resist the urge to carry on regardless and get away from it. The majority of those issues won't seem quite so much of a burden the following day. And if they are, they will be quickly resolved one way or the other – either you fix an issue, or live with it.

BUILDING A MIX

At Sun Studios, Sam Phillips had two mono tape recorders, some decent microphones, a room to put them in and not much else. What can you do with that? Put the microphones in the right place and that's about all – unless you happen to discover tape echo or Elvis, both of which Sam did, whether by design or accident. I'm afraid I must assume you're on the brink of neither. But you have completed a recording, weeded out the best takes to minimise the number of tracks and are ready to mix them into a record.

Whenever you hear a sound you've recorded for the first time, your reaction will usually be 'How can I improve it?' What about a bit of reverb, or

Allen & Heath analogue mixing desk.

EQ, or compression? Won't that help it be clearer, bigger, more authoritative, wider, punchier, more detailed? Not necessarily. What's more important and affects it the most is how it works with all the other sounds it will be combined with and the spaces between them. It's better to leave decisions on effects and cues until you have a workable balance of the whole mix, then you're able to hear how any enhancements made will actually sit in the context of everything else. You don't have to add anything at all, you know. Or sometimes, as for Sam, it's just one thing that makes all the difference.

We're going to build a mix, starting by making adjustments to the relative volumes of the tracks overall; cues and effects will be done at a later stage. Track volumes are usually located on the left-hand side of the mix window, or at the bottom of each fader.

Let's say that you've used the Glyn Johns mic array on the drums. We'll start from there.

1. Load up the kick on track one, left and right overheads on tracks two and three, and the 'if you really need it' snare on track four.
2. Pan tracks two and three at 10 o'clock and 2 o'clock respectively and get a nice natural balance between tracks one, two and three, leaving track four muted for the moment.
3. Bring in the bass on track five and add that to the balance and do the same with guitars, keyboard and any other instruments in the mix, adding and balancing each as you go. Don't take very long over it – say twenty minutes, or less. Use your intuition and do what feels right. Leave all the tracks panned to the centre, except for the drum overheads, and leave the vocals muted for now.

4. Save the mix so far as MIX 1, so that it can be recalled as needed. If you're using an analogue desk without recall, mark up your faders and make notes of what you've done. Keep your spontaneous monitor mixes/rough mixes like these – they often have a little bit of a spark to them that your 'serious' mixes don't have. They can be very good reference points to compare your finished mixes to, or revisit if you've lost your way.

5. Take a break – maybe twenty or thirty minutes – before listening to the mix again. How did it sound? Is anything too dominant? Or too quiet? If so, make adjustments to the track volumes in increments of + or –2dB, no more. Check carefully after each adjustment. Is it an improvement or not? If not, return to the level it was at. Better now? Is the mix starting to hang together well? Are all the instruments audible? Do the parts sit together naturally? Or is something in the way?

6. Ask yourself if it really needs that third guitar solo, or this or that keyboard part. Mute anything that seems to add clutter. Cross-reference by muting and unmuting overdubs if they are in question. Be brutal with any 'decorative' overdubs and keep only the essential elements. Get rid of anything that may have been fun to perform, but not to hear repeatedly.

7. After you've done all that, check the balance once more. If any of the track levels need adjustment, do it in increments of no more that + or –0.67dB. This may seem a very small and unusual amount, but it does make a big difference in fine-tuning a balance. You can actually move as little as the width of the line on a fader and make an audible difference (approximately 0.20dB). Alternatively, if you think the mix is shaping up nicely, you can leave fine-tuning until the vocals are in the picture.

8. Load up and add the lead vocal, then position it in the balance at a level that is the most consistent overall. Don't worry if there are some words that are too loud, or some that are too quiet. There will be. What you're looking for is to get a picture of the entire mix before dealing with the details, focusing on how the mix sounds with a vocal added to it. If you have an alternate take of the lead vocal, load it up and sit it in the mix at a similar level. You can make a choice on which is the winner later.

How does the balance sound now? Are the drums and bass loud enough? Or is another instrument too dominant, or too quiet? If so, make an adjustment. If it feels like a good balance except for the drums and bass, make them louder or quieter – by the same increments, if you want to keep the relationship between them.

Whenever you make a level change, be conscious of its effect on everything else. The changes you make will always have consequences, so be very aware of that when you make adjustments. Your aim at this point is to have a good representation of your mix without any effects or cues at all.

9. You've done that? Fine. Now mute the vocals and concentrate on the instrumental mix you've built. What are your impressions of it? Note where you think the shortcomings might be, and what cues you need to do. Make a detailed TBD list. Then save what you have now as MIX 2. Or if you're doing a live mix, mark up the faders accordingly.

MANUAL LEVEL ADJUSTMENTS

So far, you've made simple level adjustments to the track volumes as a whole. To manage level cues within tracks themselves, you'll likely be using faders on your control surface or mixer, or perhaps working entirely 'in the box'.

One of the more challenging aspects when mixing digitally is to change level accurately and easily within the same track. You can do this with an automated fader move, or by editing the track itself – which in some software may feel as if it takes longer than circumnavigating the globe. But

waveform

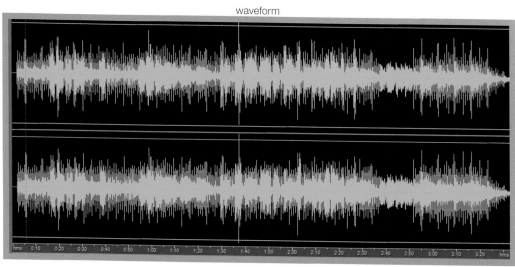

zoom

select

−2db

−4db

don't be tempted to open/copy/paste a new track to facilitate it; keeping the number of tracks to a minimum is important, whether you're working with faders or not. The greater number of tracks you have to manage, the harder it will be to cross-reference and balance across them. Ideally, all of the tracks should be visible to you without having to scroll a window back and forth, or flip to another bank of faders too often.

If you've recorded in the analogue style described in Chapter 3, you'll already have fewer tracks to deal with, but will still need to make numerous level adjustments as the mix progresses, often to peaks and transients too brief to perform with fader moves. These adjustments are best made to the track itself, which you should save as a copy when completed, for example 'Track 12 Edit.wav', so that you can go back to the original at any time. I use this 'print as you go' method for effects too. It greatly reduces processing, latency and 'digital-ness', as well as encouraging decisiveness and cross-referencing. But that's up to you. Either way, make the initial level adjustments before adding effects.

I understand why compression is so overused on digital recordings; transients and peaks are so much more apparent than with analogue, when the nature of tape compression took care of it and compressors were used more as an enhance-ment than a fix. Making manual level adjustments to a digital recording is a way to keep a natural feel to a mix and avoid overcompression. We're not aiming to smooth out a track completely, only to adjust the loudest or quietest parts, so when you do use compression it can work in the most

optimal way, without having to push too hard and squeeze the life out of a performance.

You might find some overly loud crash cymbals, vocal notes that have plosive entry points, or a small section of guitar that is too quiet. Your ears will tell you where to look when you check the balance. You don't have to solo or examine every track in the smallest detail, though I'd always recommend checking vocals, where peaks, tran-sients and overly quiet parts are most likely – and very apparent when you examine the waveform.

If your control surface has faders, you may be able to select the region you want to adjust easily. Or not – especially for fast peaks and transients. They are often too brief, or too small. When it's not straightforward to handle them with automation, or with your software if you work entirely 'in the box', you could use a free program like Audacity, where you can make accurate level adjustments more easily, then reload the adjusted track in your favoured software to continue with the mix. In a nutshell, this is how it's done:

1. Solo the track in question and examine the waveform in detail.
2. With your mouse, select the loud or quiet notes, or region you wish to adjust.
3. Click VOL (or whatever it says in your program) and type in the + or –dB you wish to change the level by.
4. Check the adjustment in context of the mix and undo/redo until correct; level adjustments should sound natural and consistent with the track, whether soloed or in context.

It will take a little practice, but you'll become adept at making spot level adjustments like these fairly quickly. It's useful to make your own presets for common level adjustments (for example, + or –0.67dB, 2dB, 4dB) to speed up the process. These are typical values to correct peaks and troughs in instruments and vocals, and for fine-tuning bumpy mixes. You will find making manual level edits like this will even out longer sections of a track that might be too loud or too quiet; for these,

OPPOSITE TOP: Waveform with one large peak.

OPPOSITE MIDDLE LEFT: Zoom in on peak.

OPPOSITE MIDDLE RIGHT: Select peak to adjust.

OPPOSITE BOTTOM LEFT: An adjustment of –2dB.

OPPOSITE BOTTOM RIGHT: An adjustment of –4dB.

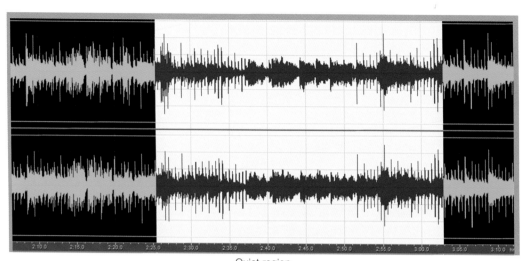

Quiet region

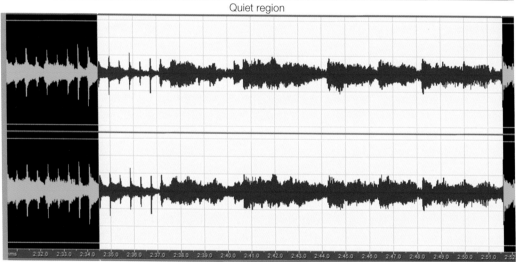

zoom

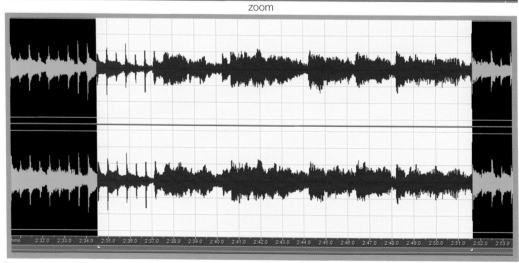

+2dB

you'd expect to use smaller amounts of gain or reduction, typically between + or −0.67 and 2dB at most. Whenever you've finished making adjustments to a track, save it as 'Track _____ edit'.

TRANSIENT PEAK EDITING

Sudden changes in loudness cause transient peaks. These are often found on vocals, cymbals and other dynamic sounds. You can identify them on a waveform as very thin lines that often stretch from edge to edge of the window. They are not always seen by compressors.

Adjusting significant peaks and dips at this point will save time locating and fixing troublesome spots as the mix progresses. Consider it

preparatory work that helps you avoid being side-tracked later. A good mix is dependent on getting the levels right, and there will be more level adjustments than anything else – especially on vocals; dealing with the biggest, most audible peaks and dips will help more than any number of plug-ins. You'll have a louder, clearer mix, effects you use will be easier to manage, and the mix will master all the better for it.

1. Solo the track and examine the waveform; the transient peaks are those very thin lines that run right to the edge.
2. Select a region with a peak and zoom in; a magnified transient peak has a triangle-like shape.
3. Select the start and end point of the triangle.

Consistent peaks, as you might find on a snare track. Each hit has its impact, but the levels are even and there is no need for adjustment.

Transient peaks are the very thinnest lines you can see on this waveform and stretch from edge to edge of the window. There are two of them shown here.

OPPOSITE TOP: A region can be as short as a single word, or as long as a verse or more. On this example, it is a section that is a little too quiet in this mix.

OPPOSITE Zoom in to select the part.

OPPOSITE BOTTOM: Shows the difference in raising the levels by +2dB. It may not seem a lot, but is just enough to make the mix flow more evenly..

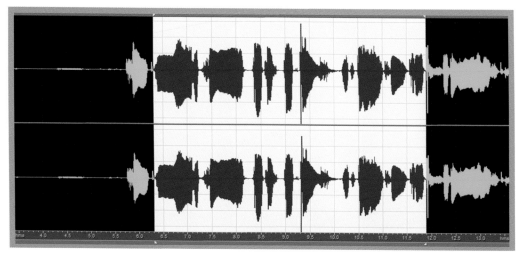

transient

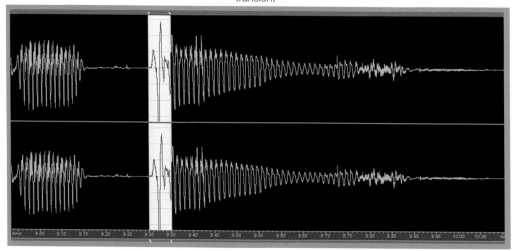

Zoom, select

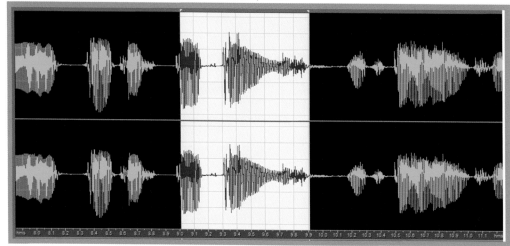

Reduction of −5dB for large fast transient

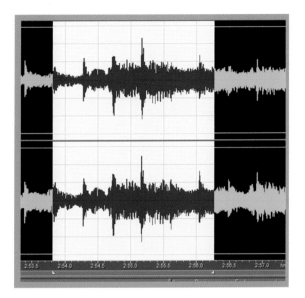

The very thin line on the waveform is a small to moderate peak.

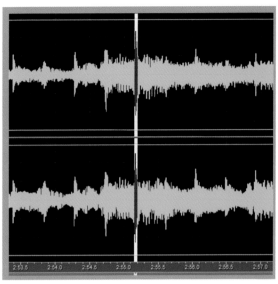

Select the peak – just the very thin line.

4. Adjust the volume by –4dB to –6dB (the actual amount will vary depending on the sound in question).
5. Zoom out and compare the level of the peak to where it was before. Does it look a similar height as the rest of the track now and sound natural when you listen? Compare by selecting a few bars prior and following the peak. There should not be a noticeable level drop. If it doesn't feel consistent, repeat the process until it sounds good in context.

Smaller transients are occasional events, not a series of peaks as you would find on a snare drum track, for example, where the impact of each snare hit is clearly visible, but evenly distributed. They are dealt with in a similar way to manual level adjustments; you're just working with much smaller regions,

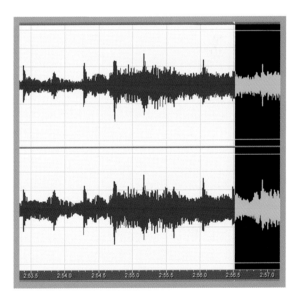

With an adjustment of –2.67dB, the small peak is no longer visible and is reduced without noticeably changing the sound.

OPPOSITE TOP: The thin line running almost edge to edge is a fast transient peak.

OPPOSITE MIDDLE: You'll see it has a triangular shape when you zoom in.

OPPOSITE BOTTOM: A level adjustment between –4 and –6dB will reduce the transient without affecting the perceived level or dynamics.

Peak editing may seem laborious, but it's worth the effort, as you don't have to use harsh compression settings – you won't lose the dynamics and sensitivity of a vocal, for example.

CUES AND FADERS

Once you've finished all that (or not!), you should have a basic instrumental balance and, broadly, the dynamics of the mix will be evident in it. You'll be aware of key level cues occurring in the arrangement – solos and other focal-point features. If you are working completely 'in the box', without faders, you should make these adjustments manually and save to the track as described, carefully cross-referencing as you go. Save them as 'Track _____ edit' when you're done. You may still have to redo some of these cues when you make final fine-tuning adjustments, but they are likely to be small ones.

If you're using a control surface with faders, or an analogue mixer, you'll be making most of your cues with them. Faders come in two varieties, long throw and short throw. You mostly find long-throw faders on analogue or more expensive mixing consoles. Most control surfaces use short-throw faders, in banks of four, eight or sixteen. Because long-throw faders are bigger, they're easier to control – simply because the gradations have wider spaces between them. But you can work effectively with short-throw faders. They just need a little more attention when it comes to fine detail. Both fader types can be marked up in exactly the same way.

Take a look at your faders, whether they're physical or on screen, and note the distance between −5dB and 0, and 0 to +5dB. They are likely to be the biggest cue distances you will use, other than for fade-outs. Usually, cues are rather less than that, so the increments can be very small. I work to the width of the line printed on a physical fader and as little as 0.20dB on a virtual one. You may prefer to make these very small adjustments by editing the waveform itself.

I'm not a big fan of automated faders; often they respond slowly, or you need to bump them to start a move. If your faders are able to move without engaging the automation, I'd opt to do that until you've rehearsed and are ready to save the cue. It's just faster doing that.

You've saved the levels of your basic balance and now you need to mark up those fader levels as your starting point, before attempting any cues. Otherwise, you will never be able to get back to where you started from. This is standard practice in analogue mixing; we used to use chinagraph pencils, now sadly obsolete. We'll use masking tape and some fine-line coloured pens. Cut fader-length pieces of masking tape, narrow enough to stick between each fader, taking care that the fader can move smoothly, then draw a line on the tape adjacent to the line on each fader of your mix balance. (If you switch between fader banks, assign a different coloured pen to each bank.) These are the levels of your initial mix balance and your reference point for the fader moves you make. That balance is a good yardstick; it was likely made in an intuitive way, with fresh ears and no overthinking. You may find yourself going back to it. Trusting your instincts usually works and it's good to keep that mentality as you work through your cues.

Start with the biggest, most obvious cues – solos, for example, and work your way down to the smaller refinements of the mix. Mark your cue points on the faders in the same way, so that you can make smooth, accurate moves, whether you use automation or an analogue mixer. Your standard mixer channel strip reads like this:

Kick / snare/ OH left /OH R/Bass / Gtr 1 / Gtr 2 / Kbd 1 / Kbd 2 / L Vox / BV 1 / BV 2.

Many fader moves will be small ones. A typical + or −5dB is only about 0.75cm ¼in) on a short-throw fader, which is a lot of level in a short distance. For fine balancing, expect cue moves of 0.40cm ($^1/_8$in), or under, for the smaller detail of a mix. You'll be amazed how very minor level

Analogue mixing, with state of the art masking-tape mix cues.

adjustments can focus and 'sit' a mix precisely. Practise fader line moves to tame subtle peaks and dips. You'll become attuned to making these small moves accurately and quite quickly – though it will feel awkward at first. Both your listening and fader skills will improve no end.

Check the master volume output level from time to time. Fader creep is very common as you adjust and add tracks to a mix, so keep an eye out for levels pushing into the red and distorting, as you work through the cues. If the mix is getting too hot, pull the master volume back accordingly.

For strong, dynamic mixes, I find my cue levels by pushing the fader up louder than it should be, then gradually pulling it back until I hear where it sits *just* so into the mix. Starting quieter and pushing the fader up can be a little tentative.

Focal points and feature cues like solos and instrumental hooks that make a statement are the most effective. As a rule of thumb, they will share a similar level to that of the vocal (roughly +5dB above the basic track). Mark the new position on the masking tape and you'll know exactly where to move that fader every time.

Note that + or –2dB is a very useful amount in judging how loud or quiet, sensitive or dominant something needs to be. Try it whenever you ask yourself, 'Is that part too loud or not?' Fine-tuning cues will be less than + or –2dB and sometimes difficult to perform accurately with a fader, so you may decide it's better to make those by editing the level of the track itself, after any effects have been applied.

A cluster of moves can happen in quick succession, or simultaneously. They are often at transition points in a song – verse to chorus, chorus to bridge, for example. You might have to ride a small fader movement several times, or move two or three faders in a few seconds. There *will* be enough time to handle everything as one pass, if you rehearse the cue well. Work to the rhythm of the track with a logical sequence of actions. Even if you are using automation, mark your fader when you are sure of the cue points; you may want to make small changes later on.

PANNING

The apparent size of a mix is much less dependent on panning than on the dynamics of a musical arrangement. But you can use panning to enhance clarity and depth as well as space; an obtrusive sound (like a sinewave synth or chainsaw guitar) can be lessened by off-centre panning. Shifts in position affect the perceived volume and sometimes a panning adjustment can be more effective than a fader level change. Note that adding stereo effects to panned tracks changes the apparent position of the instrument in proportion to the amount of effect applied.

The stereo imaging of digital is quite different from analogue. Sounds feel wider – sometimes so much that you notice 'holes' in them. On analogue, they occupy a more natural space. Here's a little trick you can try on a lead vocal; a mono signal. Copy or bounce it to make a stereo track, then put it in the centre of the mix. The nature of digital imaging will widen it very slightly and add more 'in the room' presence.

My compromise with digital imaging has been to pan closer than you might otherwise, to bind the sounds together in a cohesive way. This gives it more of an analogue character – to my ears, anyway. The maximum width I'd suggest is no more than 8 o'clock and 4 o'clock, with the main groupings between 10:30 and 2:30 and very close to centre. Typically, I might pan bass, kick, snare, vocals, rhythm guitar and a stereo keyboard to

Watkins Copicat tape delay-ay-ay.

the centre, drum overheads at 10 o'clock and 2 o'clock, with lead guitar or other features (recorded in stereo) at 9 o'clock and 3 o'clock. Of course, you can pan in a more extreme way – wider or narrower. Consider this a secure starting point.

When working with a lot of tracks, make a panning map by sketching a semicircle and marking the top as 'centre' and each end 'left' and 'right' respectively. Then play around arranging the instruments around it proportionally.

You can emphasise weight and solidity by mono or close to mono panning, or, conversely, use more extreme left to right panning combinations to create contrasts and surprise. You'll hear audacious panning on early Peter Green's Fleetwood Mac albums, Love's *Forever Changes* and The Beatles' 'White Album' and *Abbey Road*, which glues together effortlessly and is well-nigh impossible to replicate with a digital equivalent.

Keeping relatively balanced overall levels between left and right channels is important, but it is by no means a requirement that the meters should read equally at all times. In fact, if they do, the mix may be rather lacking in dynamics.

EFFECTS

At this point, we've focused on levels, level adjustments and building a solid, workable mix balance, without giving much thought to effects. There are two reasons for this. Adding an effect will change the volume level of what it's applied to, so it's easier to compensate for this when you have a decent balance to measure it against. You might also be surprised to find that you actually need fewer effects than you imagined and in smaller amounts. Well-balanced mixes simply don't need as much.

I advocate a 'print as you go' method for effects. With the vast number of plug-ins available, it's easy to drown in a sea of choices and adjustments. You risk losing sight of the mix altogether, questioning all your decisions and ending up making the wrong ones. Whether EQ, reverb, compression,

or any effect, its position in the mix and every adjustment you make to it changes the relationships between *all* of the sounds.

Use only one choice per effect you plan to use – one compressor, one limiter, one reverb, one delay, one EQ (if you *really* need it). You can adjust the settings and amounts for different elements of the mix and the characteristic will be consistent. Doing this ensures that you don't have tonal clashes or even phase cancellation by mixing and matching multiple, incompatible effects.

Take compression, for example. Solo the track of your choice and find a setting you think will work best. To check if the character of an effect you propose to use is appropriate, set the level of the effect in comparison to the signal much louder than you intend to use it. You can identify what works well much faster. Once you've chosen the effect setting, back off the amount to suit.

Then listen in context on a small section of the mix to check that you made the right call; only take a few seconds over this. If it's correct, you should know immediately. If not, adjust it and readjust a couple of times, but if you haven't got it in three, maybe try your limiter instead; don't linger over it. Effects of any kind are deceptive. It's remarkable how easily and quickly your ears become adjusted to them, especially when listening to an isolated track. With any effect, use the *least* amount you can. When you have got the sound you're looking for, apply it to the track and save it as 'track _____ comp.edit' (or whatever the effect is), then you're covered if you need to revisit it. Now, you can forget about it and move on. The benefit of 'printing as you go' is making fast decisions, instead of tweaking it for a week!

EQ
It worries me when people quote frequencies as though they were isolated, definitive things. They're not, because, like volume, any adjustments affect all the other sounds around them. Unfortunately, I will have to do just that, as I'm dis-cussing EQ.

There are two types of EQ, shelf and peak. Shelving EQ affects all the frequencies in its range – high or low for example – whereas peak EQ only affects the selected frequency. Theoretically. A parametric equaliser, as you'll find on most mixing consoles and plug-ins, has separate controls for the frequency (broken down into hi, mid and lo), the amount of boost or cut marked as + or –dB, and Q (bandwidth). Q enables variations between shelf and peak types. A small or narrow Q affects a single frequency. The wider the Q, the more frequencies are affected at either side of it.

You'll hear and read all kinds of guff about EQ. There are too many opinions on how, when or if you should use it, but there is no one right way, no one size fits all. At one time, EMI desks had just two simple EQ choices; a shelf EQ, of + or –5dB at 10kHz or 60Hz. Something like that. Not exactly a world of choice, but it didn't seem to hurt them any.

EQ is not like an effect you use to stick on in various amounts willy-nilly. Other decisions already made will have a lot of bearing on it – initial choices about instrumentation, arrangements and how you recorded the piece having the biggest consequences. The mic you used and where you placed it is a major factor in the sound you will end up with. Whether you put it 10cm or 5cm (4in or 2in) away from a guitar amplifier, if you adjust the tone of the amp or guitar, how loud it is in the room – all these things are choices you're making about the EQ and character that the guitar sound will have. You also need to consider how other instruments will affect it. Will the bass guitar mask the tone, or will it blend with the keyboard as you hoped when you come to mix. Everything affects everything else and as you position the mic, this will all be in your mind, consciously or unconsciously, based on the result you're aiming for. Remember that as you're setting mics and testing sounds. The better your judgment, the fewer problems you will encounter, the less tweaking you will need in the mix and the closer the sound will be to the way you imagined it.

You do *not* have to EQ every track. That's absolute nonsense. There is no 'Big Boys' Book of Recording' that says so. Digital EQ doesn't sound that great as a rule and you're just as likely to wreck a sound as improve it. Magnify that over each track of an entire multitrack and you're in trouble. There will be so much phase cancellation and, together with the processing footprint over multiple tracks, the mix will be thin and harsh sounding, or a ball of mush – you know what I mean. Phase cancellation is what happens when two frequencies in the same range overlap each other and make holes in the sound. The truth is that you don't have to EQ anything at all if you've got the sound right in the first place, when you recorded it.

We all need EQ from time to time, but use it only when really necessary. It's easy to think that something sounds more attractive in isolation when you boost the lows and highs and scoop out the mid-range, but in effect you're taking out 30 per cent of the total sound. And those kinds of deceptive things may happen if you don't cross-reference and compare the effect of an EQ change, as even the smallest amount of high-end boost in the wrong place can give a fizzy character to the entire mix. Ask yourself, if instead of adding 2dB at 12kHz, would 0.5dB work just as well, or would a cut at 250Hz?

Mid-range frequencies are the hardest to hear and pick apart, because that is where most of our hearing is tuned to and the most information is found. The nuances are harder to read because of this and even harder to judge in context. Adjustments are subtle, so be careful not to take a sledgehammer to them. I actually use my compressors for EQ and tone shaping, because I'm mainly mastering stereo mixes these days. By adjusting the attack and release times, I can gently tame high or and low frequencies to bring the mid-range into focus, thereby adding more presence and detail without changing the character of the mix. It works for me, but I'm not suggesting you do that; consider it a reminder that EQ does not – and should not – necessarily need to be apparent. If you find yourself boosting or cutting more than + or –2dB, you've dialled in the wrong frequency. My advice is to be very sparing and just use EQ as a correction tool to calm down a bass bulge, bring a vocal a little more to the fore, or make an occasional tonal adjustment if there's no alternative. But don't expect it's going to improve anything radically – unless you have oodles of dosh to spend on an outboard Neve, old Pultec, Focusrite Reds, GML or whatever. The digital stuff doesn't have that kind of mojo.

EQ is a delicate beast. Poke it with a big stick at your peril – it is not forgiving if you do. So, if in doubt, don't EQ at all. And don't forget that lots of things are not actually EQ issues; often, they are more to do with level (plosives, for example), overall balance, or the musical arrangement. Subtractive EQ might clean up low-end muddiness, but it won't fix an inappropriate bass part, or one that is too loud.

COMPRESSION AND LIMITING

Ask, first of all, 'Do I really need to compress this sound?' You're not compelled to do so. Compression and limiting tame volume peaks and dips, and enhance the dynamic qualities of a recording. Or at least this is what compression is supposed to do. It's often used when tracking, again on mixdown, and yet again when mastering. It can be subtle and transparent, or quite audibly pumping holes in the sound, whether gently or aggressively. Be aware that compression will noticeably change the sound to which it's applied to some degree.

The different brands and types on offer vary tremendously in character and effectiveness. There are hundreds of software compressor/limiter plug-ins to choose from, be they from well-established manufacturers, or obscure, one-man designers. The analogue-style plug-ins usually feature a retro-looking interface, somewhat simpler to navigate than the modern brick-wall or multiband types. Tonality is the main thing, that is, whether the footprint of a compressor is sympathetic to the sounds to which it's applied. Always try before you buy. Don't bother unless you can have a decent free trial, then make sure that you

download direct from the manufacturer/designer to avoid catching any bugs.

You don't need a big variety of different compressors, regardless of all those companies who make claims that you should just get this one or that one, and then all your mixes will be wonderful. Rubbish. It's a real 'Emperor's new clothes' area. Settle on just one or two compressors with good sonic qualities and stick with them; it will take time to understand them well. Avoid multiband compression – it's an invention of the devil and the destroyer of many a mix. It will radically change the EQ as well and that's the last thing you want after working hard to get a good sound to begin with. Any compression affects the EQ of a track in subtle ways, sometimes pleasantly, sometimes not. So choose carefully.

A compressor reduces the volume of some, or all, of the sound, evening it out to make a vocal or mix 'sit' better, while adding punch and clarity to drums, bass or other instruments. By reducing the volume of the loudest parts and boosting the quieter ones, the signal is more defined and 'present', with the lumps and bumps ironed out. But don't expect compression/limiting to make a vocal completely smooth and even – it won't. Big peaks and dips are mainly due to the nature of digitally recorded sound, or poor mic technique on the part of the vocalist. A little compression or limiting will enhance a vocal that is delivered well, but always expect to make some manual level adjustments too.

It's hard to 'hear' compression at first – so the tendency is to overdo it. It's not always easy to detect the effects of it, especially when used lightly, so practice is needed to get to grips with the controls, which are interdependent. Plug-in presets occasionally point you in the right direction and are not a bad starting point, but the effects of compression are unique to the signal going through it. You have to find your own way and deal with each sound on its own merits to a large extent.

'Ratio' sets the amount of compression. 'Threshold' is simply how much of it you want,

'Attack', how quickly you want it to respond, while 'Release' controls how long you want it to hold on for. Make good use of the 'Bypass' button, to compare the compressed signal with the original. Adjust the 'Output' so that both are at a very similar volume level, otherwise the volume difference – or perceived volume difference – will be misleading.

My Compressor Tendencies

Note that the settings are very variable!

- Instruments/vocals – a fairly fast attack/release, and low threshold, 2:1 ratio
- Mastering – very slow or moderate attack, fast release, low threshold and ratio.

NEVER run your compressor over the mix bus or stereo output. If you do, it will play havoc with your mix balancing and be a real liability when the mix needs to be mastered.

A limiter is basically a stronger, faster type of compressor. It's useful to have a limiter on hand to reach the places a compressor can't always reach, as they're well suited to sounds with a wide dynamic range, vocals or drums. Sometimes, your compressor of choice will be bundled with a limiter, or have a limiter setting. Or you may prefer to use a limiter with a slightly different characteristic.

Tape compression, lovely as it is, can only be achieved with analogue tape recorders. The process of recording to magnetic tape squashes signal peaks in a way that is very sympathetic to the recorded material and attractive to the ear. People talk about analogue being 'warm' due to valves in the equipment and whatnot, when what they are actually referring to is tape compression. But the sound of tape was not just the tape recorder in itself (although they all had their own characteristics). The console, preamps, transformers and wiring in the old studios also played a big part in

the effect, as did the engineers, producers and artists working in them. Of course you can use a tape recorder or cassette in your signal chain and feed everything through it – but you'll wonder what happened to the high end and why the lows have disappeared!

Reverb and Delay

Think of reverb as the space that sounds travel through. It is cumulative. Each additional instrument you have bouncing around in the space makes new reflections and the way these reflections behave in any given room defines its acoustics.

In the analogue era, all reverb came from a physical echo chamber, an echo plate, spring, or some kind of tape delay, as well as later outboard equivalents such as the Space Echo, Lexicons and so on, all of which were very functional. The digital plug-in equivalents are based on the same principles, but behave a little differently. Overall, the imaging is wider, the decays trickier to blend and they can feel 'stuck on' at times. But they are usable enough, if not tweaked unduly.

The biggest mistake with reverb is to think that it needs to go on everything so as to make the recording seem 'real'. Typically, in the old studios, the rooms were big, with well-designed acoustics, so the sound of musicians playing in them was already enhanced by the room and needed little more. The reverb or delay would often be used only on vocals or featured instruments. This is worth remembering. Even in a scenario where instruments have been recorded in a small space, reverb and/or delay applied to only the vocal creates an illusion that there is reverb on everything else. Try it and see if you don't believe me – set up your vocal reverbs before the instruments.

You *don't* need reverb on everything. It should be used selectively and carefully, or your mix will be unfocused and confusing. And even more so, if you mix and match different reverb settings or types within the same mix. One reverb (albeit in different amounts) and one delay are sufficient.

For a classic, analogue-style reverb, use large room sizes and longer time settings, but with short decays and a minimal wet/dry mix. A delay behind the reverb will make it deeper or wider. A mono, Watkins Copicat type of delay (or even a Space Echo) is more manageable than a multitap delay, which is far too busy and lacks a certain randomness that lends authenticity to it. Sometimes you will find a tape-style delay itself is all the reverb you need.

Back when dinosaurs ruled the Earth, this was called Tape Echo, because it was made by, er … tape recorders. You can use it on its own, or in conjunction with reverb. Adding a delay will make the reverb sound MUCH bigger. It can be quite effective to use a smaller reverb with delay added, rather than a big reverb. The reflections are more controllable and you can create the effect of a large reverb in a much cleaner way.

A subtle delay tucked behind vocals and lead instruments will add depth and dimension; overt delay will give space and distance. Close delays, sometimes with only a single repeat, create that bathroom-style, rock 'n' roll, slapback echo, and when the timing is very, very close to the signal with a single repeat, you get ADT (artificial double tracking), which thickens the texture of sounds.

Take care with stereo digital delays, as they're hard to control and usually more effective without any reverb added to them. A delay can add space and dimension if used well, but it's easily overdone. Mono delay is best, unless you're running Ping Pong Ball Studios.

OTHER EFFECTS

There are more effects out there than you can shake a bundle of sticks at; you name it, there's an effect for it. Effects in themselves never fix anything, or mask a mistake. But, on occasion, some special effects can be handy, when they are justified in the context of, and specific to, the material. That's fine; anything well thought out and imaginative always is. But many are just tiresome ideas that are there for the sake of it and are time-wasters for all concerned.

THE INSTRUMENTAL MIX

Your level cues are done and saved. Now, mute the vocal and review the instrumental mix. Listen closely to the bass. Is it sitting consistently in the mix, or does it feel a little uneven at times? Check if you notice too much resonance on the lowest notes, or other unwelcome tonal changes. If you feel it lacks punch, or is not smooth or consistent enough, solo it and take a look at the waveform. Do you notice a lot of noticeably big peaks? Or just a few? If there are only a few, zoom in on each and adjust the volume down by −4dB. Does it look a similar height as the rest of the bass track now and sound natural? Compare by selecting a few bars prior and following the peak, then readjust the level as needed. There should not be an apparent drop in level. You can also use this technique to tame resonant low notes that don't register as a peak, by selecting the whole note and reducing by −2dB.

If there are a large number of peaks, they will be better dealt with by some compression or limiting. Be relatively gentle with the settings and cross-reference closely with both the uncompressed track and the mix itself. When using compression, you'll likely find that the level you set in the mix will need adjustment to match up and blend as it did before. So always note its original level so that you can get back to where you started if necessary. Do this whenever you use compression on an entire track; sometimes it just doesn't sit well with everything else, even if the levels match up.

After listening in context, is the level even, with enough clarity? If it's lumpy or resonant, change the compression, using a faster attack. Keep a fast release, until it comes into focus and is more distinct. Alternatively, if it is very uneven, try a limiter instead. It will react to frequent, bigger peaks more quickly.

Once the bass is to your liking, take a quick check on the drums. Is the kick at the right level? Are there many peaks and dips? Manually adjust significant ones, or compress if inconsistent throughout. If you are using the fourth 'optional' snare mic, check and adjust in the same way. Loud cymbal crashes are best dealt with by spot level adjustments. The attack of the crash is where all the energy lies. You might try handling it as you would a vocal peak edit, but a little more gently; but don't forget that the overhead mics affect the entire kit! If the overheads are uneven, add a little compression if you really have to, but be very careful not to overdo it.

Check the relationship between the kick and the bass. Do they blend and work together well tonally with each other, as good or better than before? If not, check that the balance is correct, or adjust any compression you may have used on them.

For the most part, the following applies to both electric and acoustic guitars. Check for any major peak edits or volume adjustments on lead guitar solos, or single-note riffs. More punch can be achieved with a little compression or limiting, but don't squash the dynamics too much. Moderate compression can add a bit more weight and definition for rhythm guitars, especially on a weak player. Try a medium>fast attack, and a fairly fast release, with a 2:1 ratio. But make any manual level adjustments first. Be wary of adding reverb to a rhythm guitar, as it might result in creating rhythmic conflicts or mask other sounds. If you want to add presence and depth, these can sometimes benefit from a delay, rather than reverb.

Keyboards are more than likely to be electronically generated sounds. Most are best left alone, though some might need a small amount of reverb to make them blend more naturally in the mix. Use the same reverb as the vocal, but in a different amount. Using just one type of reverb in a mix is enough. For a John Lennon style piano sound, use a single repeat, mono delay. If you have an acoustic piano, some compression can bring it to the fore, especially for more rhythmic parts.

Check other instruments in the same manner – adjust significant peaks or level discrepancies and be very sparing with any effects. Once the instrumental cues are complete, save as 'MIX 3'. Then you're ready to add vocal tracks to the picture.

VOCALS

The lead vocal is the main focal point for the listener and they need to hear it. Don't be shy with the level; get it as loud as you can without it feeling inconsistent, or 'stuck on' to the mix.

VOCAL LEVELS

You'll make more level adjustments to vocals than anything else. A compressor won't fix everything; consider it more as an enhancement. You may find a combination of compressor and a limiter is more effective. It all depends on the vocals, but make a few manual adjustments before you do either.

On occasion, you will encounter plosives. They tend to occur on Ps, Bs and other hard syllables, or when a vocalist is too near the mic. They make uncomfortable pops, bulges and, sometimes, level clipping. You can contain them with careful level editing. They won't disappear completely, but in context will be much less noticeable, or will be completely hidden by other sounds in the mix.

Looking at the diagrams, you'll note that only the thinnest (loudest) part of the plosive is selected. If this is not effective, select a slightly wider area to contain the plosive. For low-frequency plosives, also select the two biggest peaks on either side.

When you set a vocal level, it may seem natural to use the loudest parts as your guide. Don't. Use the quietest, or you will almost certainly end up with some syllables disappearing. Look at the waveform overall first; you'll see the most apparent peaks and dips at a glance. Look for the biggest transient peaks to begin with. These are often at the start of a word. Adjustments might be as little as –2dB, or as much as –6dB. Be sure to cross-reference level changes with the mix, especially when dealing with plosives or sibilance, which always sound much worse in isolation than they do in context.

Once you've dealt with the transients, you may find that a vocal has some words which are too prominent, or too quiet, on playback, even if you

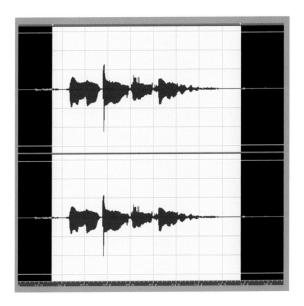

Plosive.

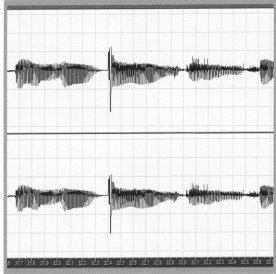

Zoom in.

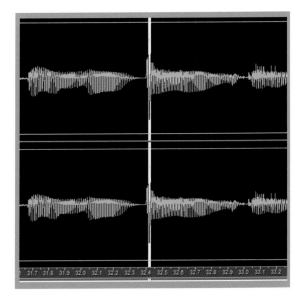

Select.

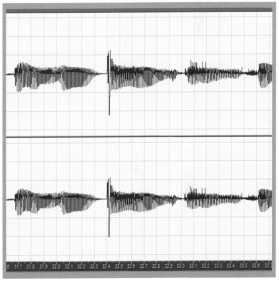

Adjustment of –6dB.

have applied compression or limiting. This is to be expected. Locate the quietest parts, often soft syllables at the start or end of a line. They'll benefit from a boost, starting with +2dB, sometimes more. Check that adjustments sound natural and

are of a similar level to the adjoining syllable. Likewise, adjustments of –2dB can work just as well for small bulges or overly loud syllables.

If there are longer sections of a vocal that need attention, for example a repair line that is too quiet

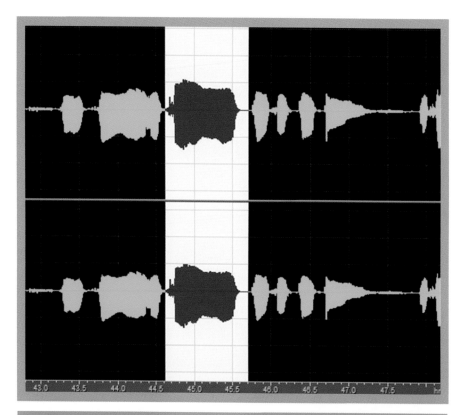

A loud syllable – just enough to make a little bulge in the vocal track.

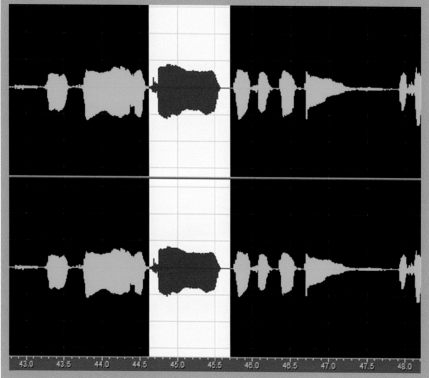

With a level reduction of −2dB, the level is gently evened out. You can fine-tune any sound, down to 0.67dB or even lower, but always base your decision on what you hear – not what you see on a waveform.

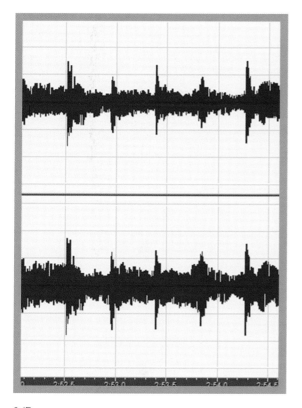

0dB.

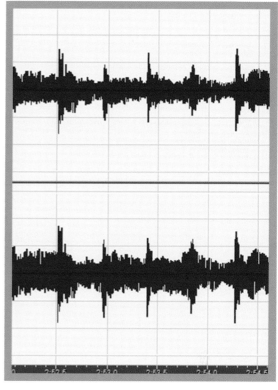

+0.67dB.

or loud in relation to the rest, adjustments are usually small ones; + or –2, 1.33, or even 0.67dB. Making small adjustments will sound more 'real' than leaving a compressor to take care of it.

A vocal needs some ebb and flow so that the emotional quality of the performance comes across effectively. Even the heaviest rock record needs this in some small way. Whatever the style of the record, when you put the vocal in context with the track, set the overall level by the quietest part. This will always show up any unduly loud words, which you can then adjust as needed. But don't get your head stuck in too many very small adjustments, or you'll catch 'Manual Compression Syndrome'!

When you've completed the level adjustments, you should add the effects you plan to use. Most commonly it will be compression/limiting, reverb/delay. I'd avoid EQ if you possibly can, unless there's a very specific problem. Minor issues can

often be addressed in the way you set a compressor or limiter: a fast attack/release will reduce low frequencies; a slower attack/release will tame the high end, without overtly changing the character of the sound. Likewise, the reverb you choose will affect the tonal qualities of the vocal. When using more than one effect, the order they're processed in also makes a difference to the result, so check whether comp>reverb, or reverb>comp, works best, for example. Test the amount of each effect you use in the context of the mix, as you don't want a reverb that spills over everything else too much, or one that is too dry to be heard. Small changes to the amount of the effect applied can have a big impact.

To find the best position for a vocal in the mix, bring the vocal up louder than it needs to be, then carefully bring it down until it feels about right. Mark that spot, then listen to the track from start to finish. Does the vocal feel consistent? Can you hear all the words? If a vocal is too quiet overall, it will sound like it's fighting with the rest of the mix. Few mixes suffer from vocals being too loud. The overall level should feel natural, apart from obviously loud or quiet notes, which you can attend to as cues or manual adjustments.

A trick to check the relative level of the vocal is to turn down the monitors, plug in headphones, put them on the floor, then play back. If it's positioned well, the vocal will be easily audible and feel comfortable in the balance. If you're in doubt about whether a vocal is too loud or too quiet, run secondary mixes, one with the vocal +0.67dB and another with the vocal at −0.67dB. Come back a day later and listen to all three mixes. One of them will answer the question.

There is just +0.67dB between the two waveforms in the images and the difference is hardly visible. The second waveform has a volume adjustment of +0.67dB. Look closely. Open a waveform and select a small portion. Play back, then increase the volume by +0.67dB. Undo and redo to compare the difference between them, then do the same, with a level change of −0.67dB. It's a very effective measurement for fine-tuning mixes, taming small peaks, or adding just a little more presence to quiet parts.

Backing Vocals
Harmony or backing vocals don't usually need quite so much attention as a lead vocal. Check and adjust peaks and dips, using the same effects as on the lead vocal, but in different amounts; possibly with slightly different settings if another vocalist is doing the parts. Generally, sit a high harmony vocal a little behind the lead vocal and in a similar position for three-part harmonies, with the low harmony a little louder than a high one. When you have all the vocals in place on the mix, save it.

FOCAL POINTS

What are the focal points of a mix and why are they needed? Focal points draw a listener into a mix and hold their attention while you lead them through it. Vocals, of course, are always a focal point, but you also need to make strong statements elsewhere. These can be the riffs on an intro, changes in mood and arrangement as a song moves from verse to chorus, loud to soft, dark to light, instrumental breaks and solos – these provide continual interest and are the highlights and surprises that keep a listener involved from start to finish. Strong parts are the main thing. Don't start off with guitar strumming for eight bars, or have a long preamble before anything happens; it's boring. Ideally, you're aiming to create memorable focal points throughout. Be bold and don't be timid with volume; as a rule of thumb, focal points should be as loud as the vocal.

The strength of the musical arrangement is the backbone of a good mix. A well thought-

Spoken Word Recordings

Somehow, I've always had a soft spot for spoken word recordings. The old Argo label set the benchmark for them. Argo releases had a wonderful, 'in the room with you' characteristic and were made with a quiet simplicity.

Language is the most direct method of communication for us, whether you're listening to the news, or buying a pint of milk at the shop. So when you record speech, the words must be clear and easily understood, or the message is lost. A spoken word recording could be no more than a lone voice, or might feature sound effects, a music track, or other voices in the mix.

However it pans out, always make a spoken vocal track louder than you think it should be; it's all too easy to bury. Adding another 5dB on it wouldn't hurt. It's the message that's important.

out arrangement almost mixes itself, with often a single component that governs the dynamics. This could be as simple as a guitar that is muted in the verse, opening out to full chords for choruses, or as complicated as an orchestral crescendo.

Should you find yourself with a bewildering number of cues (other than vocals), or a lacklustre, linear mix, it's likely that these dynamic focal points are lacking in the arrangement and, in their absence, you have to find an equivalent to use in the mix that offers interest and development. Be sure that you've taken out all the things you don't need, as clutter is the usual problem. See what you can subtract at various points to create light and shade. You can add clarity and definition to a mix just by muting a couple of unnecessary over-dubs. Soft and loud dynamics and contrast are as important as changing tonal values, so check the track layout for something to feature or remove in the weak spots. Don't be shy of making extreme changes, as they may surprise you.

FINE-TUNING

When your mix is nearing completion, you can feel it. Take enough time rehearsing cues and adjustments, but not too much. Quit when you feel confident in the balance, or get the sense that you're 'in the moment' and getting a buzz out if it. Try to capture that. Resist the temptation to carry on making a few more tweaks – save it! Personally, I know a mix is there when my intuition takes over and I'm *almost*, but not quite, certain of what I'm doing – it's a good place to be for that little extra something in feel or dynamics.

If you ever feel you're losing the mix, that nothing is working and none of it makes sense any more, stop. Go back to your previous move (or cluster of moves) and take a fifteen-minute break. Turn the monitors down a little, then listen again – you may be able to pick it up. If not, and you're ready to give up, leave all the effects and panning as they are and zero all the faders. Go back to the last saved version you were content with and rebalance from

scratch. It won't take anywhere near as long as you expect and the mix will be back under your control before you know it.

Once you think the mix is right, save it, and come back tomorrow – or the day after that. Always make a record of your final mix positions for faders, EQ and effects. It's not uncommon to revisit a mix, or later wonder 'How did I do that?' Spend a few minutes when you're done taking detailed notes.

Be sure to have fresh ears and as much objectivity you can muster when checking your work. Listen on your studio monitors and in one or two different rooms on different sound systems. Don't stop to check if you hear any errors, just note anything that concerns you, plus your first impressions. There will always be something you don't like, whether it's a bad cue, a balance mistake, or the sounds themselves. Some of these problems will be in your head. The likelihood is that you will think the mix is either better, or worse, than it actually is. You need to separate yourself enough from what you've done to know what the truth is.

Sometimes, listening to your original 'MIX 1' will tell you how closely you've captured what your instincts were, or how far you deviated from them. The mix might be much better than you first thought, with maybe one or two obvious things to correct; or it's a total washout and you decide start over. Either way, you'll know what to do.

EDITING

When tape was the order of the day, every engineer had to get to grips with the risky job of painstakingly locating edit points with a chinagraph pencil, scrubbing the reels back and forth by hand, physically cutting up performances, then sticking it all back together again while hoping the edits would be clean and inaudible. You rarely got the chance to undo errors; as a rule, edits were permanent. On occasion, it could be very challenging, especially where editing multitrack tape was concerned. Mess that up and you had a big

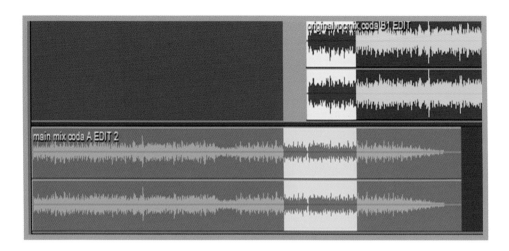

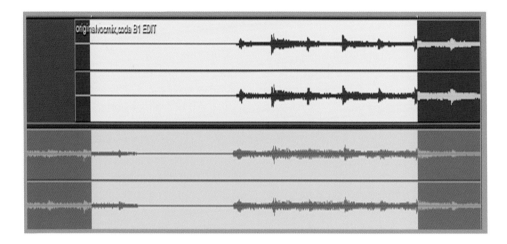

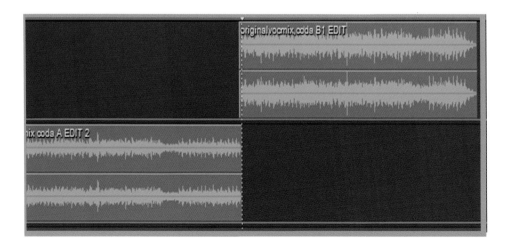

problem. One of my engineers once fixed a click on the 2in 24-track by taking his best guess as to where the offending click would be found in relation to the head block (track 17 as I remember), then cutting a tiny window in the tape to remove it. Brian Wilson reputedly spent six months chopping and changing and choosing excerpts from the dozens of mixes, submixes, keepers and outtakes that were stuck together to make *Good Vibrations.*

And the great Ken Scott made his mixes in a series of sections, stopping the tape each time he made a mistake, retaking and correcting it, then continuing on until the next error. When he'd finished, all the pieces were assembled into the final mix. Old-school recording engineers were experts at that, even though physically editing

tape was nowhere near as simple as digital. Play close attention to *Strawberry Fields Forever* and you can hear the joins, though the edit points were so carefully chosen that the audible edit actually enhanced it. Clever stuff.

Digital editing is absolutely great, because it's non-destructive. Being able to chop and change at will, undo and redo effortlessly as many times as you like, is marvellous. It has the capability to do things which would have been impossible in analogue days.

Editing may seem a bit tricky at first, until you get the hang of it. But actually, it's quite simple – you just zoom in on the waveform, find the start and end points of where you want to make the edit and cut to the beat. Sometimes it's a little more complicated, of course, and you have to

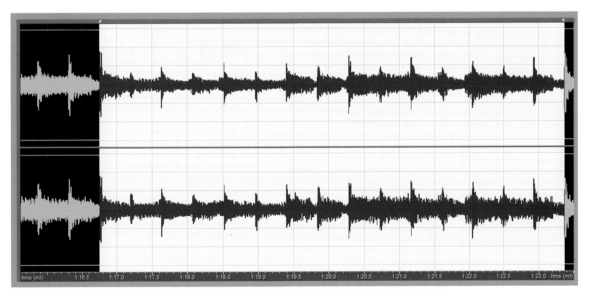

Selecting straight cut front and end edit points in a stereo mix; seamless cuts are made from edge to edge of the beats, without the need for cross-fades.

OPPOSITE TOP: The lower track shows the original mix and the upper track a submix for an alternative coda, lined up close to where the edit needs to be.

OPPOSITE MIDDLE: Zoom in to line up the edit points precisely.

OPPOSITE BOTTOM: The lower track is silenced or deleted after the edit point. Check that the levels of both tracks are matched and that the edit is seamless, then simply bounce both tracks into a new stereo mix. You can use this technique to insert alternatives or submixes anywhere within a mix.

freestyle a bit to make it seamless. Just pay attention to locate really accurate cues. Making straight cuts in the right places will always work. Avoid cross-fades; they mush up the sound and blur the joins. Well, I can hear that they do. Having to do a cross-fade means you chose the wrong edit points.

It's very useful to add editing to your toolbox. For example: you've made a small error, but the rest of the mix is fine. Maybe there's a missed cue, or an adjustment to the balance or effects level you want to make. Or you might have part of a mix that doesn't quite work, so you want to replace a particular section. Instead of remixing the entire track, make a secondary submix of the place you want to repair, then edit it in after the fact. If you want to try alternate settings on just part of a mix, make a submix of it right after the main mix (so that all the levels and settings remain the same), then edit it in later. It's a tried and tested method and works well. Give yourself enough space for easy edit points before and after the cue. And if you're making submixes, don't change the master output volume of the mixing session, or the levels won't match up!

Sometimes you can improve a stereo mix with a bit of judicious editing; replacing a weak chorus with a stronger one, tightening up or changing the structure, even reshaping it into a 'remix' version by assembling a series of submixes. Once you've learned how to edit, it opens up all sorts of possibilities.

MIXING IN MONO

Mixing in mono is far more difficult at first than stereo. There's nowhere to hide! You can't get away with any questionable EQ or levels, or use panning for space and depth. If you have a stereo/mono button, use it. It's indispensable for cross-referencing mix balances and shows up poor placement immediately. And it's especially good for checking vocal levels. Mono mixes can be extremely punchy and direct, with lots of energy. Don't assume stereo is always better, it isn't. I've often repanned a stereo mix to mono for more life and immediacy, whilst leaving reverb in stereo to keep the illusion of width – *cheat*!

PERFORMANCE MIXING

One of the biggest freedoms of analogue mixing was because there was no fiddling or fixing later. Either you got it right or got it wrong – in which case you lived with the shortcomings, or pulled down the faders and started again.

Performance mixing – live, in real time, without automation – requires decisiveness, boldness, acute timing and a seat of your pants risk-taking that just doesn't happen when you have the cosy safety net of total recall, or indeed any recall. A mix becomes a different animal altogether. Your fader moves become a choreography, a living, breathing, instinctive thing, and the choices you make will not be the same.

If you've integrated an analogue mixer, or your system allows, try it sometime – it's liberating and creative. See how easy it is to cross-reference the relationships from track to track. Set up your balance, rehearse your cues and go for it. Let your intuition take over and feel the dynamics in the same way as you would play an instrument. The cue points marked on your faders are your fall-back position, approximately. You'll find yourself nudging the positions and coaxing those cues as the mix comes into focus.

- Take one will be the tidiest, but you've probably messed up a couple of cues.

- Take two is more unruly in places, but those cue points felt better, so mark them up.

- Take three either threw caution to the wind and was a lot of fun but not really useable, or you felt focused, connected, very much in control and totally nailed it.

You might want to call it quits after three takes and edit the best bits together!

MASTERING

Mastering is often referred to as a Black Art, not easily understood by the uninitiated. Even after they've attended a mastering session in person. In a way, it's just knowing when a mix sounds like a record.

In the vinyl era, mastering engineers were responsible for cutting the master lacquers from tape. There was a simple objective; to cut the disc from the master tape as faithfully as possible. EQ was used only to correct any shortcomings in the mix, or in the acoustics of the studio it had been recorded in. Compression or limiting was added to ensure that the cut was accurate and loud enough to minimise surface noise on the vinyl as much as possible. Prior to the final cut, test lacquers were made (acetates) for record execs and the producer/artist to approve, none of whom would be expected to attend the mastering session. It was thought of as a technical rather than a creative process. Interestingly, at Abbey Road, trainee engineers started off in the mastering room, working their way up to tape op and beyond. I think that was a really good move – a fantastic way to train a novice how to listen. Once you can do that, you can handle anything.

When you master a mix, how do you get the best out of it? Traditionally, it's a combination of EQ and compression and/or a limiter applied to a mix, so that it sounds as convincing as it can possibly be. Ideally, the same – but *better*. I can

tell what's wrong with a mix and what needs to be done to rectify, fix and enhance it, without even listening to it all the way through. I know when a compression setting is right and can sense where the 'sweet spot' is, like the last piece of a jigsaw falling into place, or hearing when an instrument is in tune. I just feel it.

Don't be surprised if you struggle with mastering at first. I'd been recording for more years than you'd care to remember before I attempted to master a track. Be confident in your mixing skills first and let someone else master a few of your tracks; watch them as they work. See what they do and how they do it. The results might sound unfamiliar to you when you listen back, or be noticeably better immediately – remember you've become used to listening to your mixes multiple times and your mastering guy has fresh ears (well, if he's any good he has). Take some time to mull over how well he did.

You'll need complete objectivity to master your own stuff and will really have to step back if you intend to try, or the likelihood is that you'll make it sound worse than it was before you started. When you're ready to have a go, just think of mastering as way of bringing the most out of a mix, optimising it as far as it allows you to on a single stereo track. There are two objectives: to correct and to enhance. Often they work in tandem, but always check if there are significant corrective issues first. Simple things like poor balances are best dealt with in the mix. Mastering can only fix a bad one

Acetates from Abbey Road, Pye, Utopia and a record booth on Southport bus station.

to a limited extent, but is very adept at levelling out inconsistencies and adding more presence, detail and character across a mix as a whole.

You need to switch from active to passive listening very quickly when mastering and make decisions fast. But, most of all, you have to remain objective. Take your best shot and always compare it in the cold light of day – at the same volume as the original mix. Is it better or not? That's the only question to answer.

You may misjudge it at first, but over time the way that you 'hear' mastering will improve. Often, the adjustments you make will be very subtle, so learn to work in the smallest gradations your equipment allows. For example, my main compressor can be adjusted in increments as small as two decimal points; I can change the 'Threshold' and 'Release' from 1.24 to 1.25, 1.26 and so on, and hear the difference. It makes a difference and is the complete opposite to slamming a mix as hard as you can. Get to know your mastering compressor really well. Take a test track and push it in every direction you can. See how far you can go before it sounds horrible, as well as how seemingly small adjustments can really hit the spot, and the way the compressor changes the EQ with the settings you choose and the amount of compression you apply. EQ of any kind will have a big footprint, so make sure that it is an attractive one.

Modern-day mastering has evolved into an extension of mixing (sometimes to an alarming degree – mastering from stems is mixing!). Or, more accurately, it has evolved into a process to correct the shortcomings of a mix and *then* enhance it as much as possible. I don't want even to get into the 'loudness' issue – that's all hogwash, end of – and I will never compromise a master to satisfy the likes of Spotify, YouTube, or anyone else. A mix or a master can only be as loud as it wants to be. That is, as loud as it allows without wrecking it.

Louder is not always better and it's largely overlooked that radio stations – and online platforms – have all run some kind of compression or algorithm to equalise the programme material at a more or less similar volume. They've always done that. If you've got an overly compressed Black Metal track, it will be squashed even more to back off the volume enough to balance somewhat with the other material that is played alongside it. To cut through well for broadcast, you have to consider perceived volume, not just more level.

Perceived volume is just as important as how it reads on the meters, as anyone who's mastered a compilation album can confirm. I've lost count of the number of loud guitar-based mixes that sounded timid and weedy next to quite quiet acoustic tracks. Why? It's partly to do with how well they've been recorded and mixed, of course, but also about the tonal values and dynamics of the arrangements. Guitars going at full pelt all the time can sound flat and one-dimensional next to an authoritative rhythm section with acoustic guitar and vocals to the fore. When there is more tonal contrast and light and shade in the mix that a mastering compressor can respond to, it will cut through more strongly.

Mastering any album or compilation means taking care that the individual tracks flow evenly from one song to the next. They're not just set at the same volumes as each other. Levels are shaped from track to track to be as effective as possible given the running order. I think that's the hardest part to get right and I can easily spend more time on that than adjusting mastering settings.

Volume is deceptive and nothing can be louder than the quietest track. It might sound perverse and counter-intuitive to say so, but it's true. The quietest track dictates the maximum level to which you can go before it will be out of place in context of the others. It ruins the listening experience if one track is 2dB quieter than the rest. So why not make the quietest track louder? You probably could and it often happens, but you can only go so far without overcompressing. It is nit-picky stuff when 0.20dB makes a difference and I've spent much more time than I would like trying to persuade quiet tracks to give me a little more level without damaging them.

Mastering isn't really a Black Art. But it's nice when someone asks you to work your magic!

Mastering for Vinyl

Vinyl is organic. I don't know whether it's intentional, or just pure instinct, that an LP's playing time per side averages twenty-two minutes. That happens to be the length of the average person's optimal concentration span. It's a curious coincidence. In practical terms, I expect it probably evolved from the length of a symphony, with the four movements split evenly over both sides. There's a correlation between those two facts that might explain one aspect of vinyl's longevity: *it's the right length*.

This suits recording artists too; a 7in single or EP makes a definitive statement, when a one-sided digital download is not quite enough. To deliver a seventy-minute CD album is a real stretch – even fifty minutes is pushing it. But forty minutes, split in two twenty-minute self-contained episodes, and this little bear's porridge will be just right!

There are a few things to note when mastering for vinyl:

- Sub-bass frequencies are problematic and should be adjusted, preferably in the mix, rather than at the mastering stage.
- Appropriate compression/limiter settings will naturally pull in the imaging of mixes with wide panning very slightly and even mixes with bass or drums predominately to one side will be fine as long as the mix is a well-balanced one.
- The other main issue to be aware of is to make sure that the cutting engineer knows that the track is already mastered and to remove any high-, low-pass or other filters they might usually apply. Most pressing plants have filters set as default, so as to prevent loud peaks that can damage the cutting head (they don't come cheap!). Generally, the cutting engineer will do as you ask, if your credentials are credible. It's important to note that I never master to 100 per cent of peak volume, but at –0.20dB under.

And I'm happy with a quieter cut if the record needs it.

THE RUN-OUT GROOVE

Tempting as it may be, it does you no good to compare your own work with your favourite records or current hits. It's impossible to be truly objective, or to make a direct comparison. You can only succeed by being yourself and doing the best you're capable of. If you're happy with your work, it is good work. Commercial success is a completely different matter and nothing to do with if your work is good or bad. The divide between success and failure is paper thin and the planets all need to align, just so. And if they do, it won't be like you think!

I'll leave you with a recent record of my own – *A Tour Of British Duck Ponds*, which uses all the techniques described in this book. It was made entirely 'in the box', with obsolete software, no faders to play with and just one £15 mic. I admit to including many of the mistakes on purpose, but did spend some time getting the levels right. It is all yours at https://thinklikeakey.com or https://franashcroft.bandcamp.com.

A Tour Of British Duck Ponds.

GLOSSARY

Acetate A test pressing of a vinyl lacquer disc in use until the late 1970s, made for the approval of the record by the label and artist. The sound deteriorated badly after a few plays, so decisions had to be made quickly.

Acoustics The sound, and the behaviour of sound, within any given environment.

Active listening Critical listening, which focuses not only on individual sounds, but also their relationship with one another.

A/D converter Device to convert an analogue audio signal into a digital one.

Analogue A sound recording process in which an audio input is converted into an analogous electrical waveform. Now, is that clear, everyone?

Arrangement map A breakdown of a musical arrangement and cues according to the structure of the recording.

Artist Musicians and vocalists who perform in recording. They can be blamed if things go horribly wrong.

Baffle Any item used to eliminate or reduce sound spillage from one microphone to another.

Balance The relative volume levels of recorded tracks with each other.

Bit depth/sample rate The resolution of digital audio. The higher the bit depth and sample rate, the better the sound. Theoretically.

Bleed Spillage of sound between microphones.

Bouncing tracks Combining a number of individual tracks into a mono or stereo mix; the term can refer to compiled performances of an instrument or vocal, or all the tracks comprising a mix.

Brainstorming a session Planning, imagining and strategising a recording using free association for inspiration.

Brickwall compression A compressor or limiter used on the maximum possible setting, which crushes the signal to the point of, or beyond, the level of distortion.

Clipping Digital distortion created when sound levels exceed peak volume, that is, when the meters are in the red.

'Close your eyes and point technique' An intuitive method of microphone placement.

Compression An analogue or digital device that reduces the peaks and boosts the dips in a signal, to enhance or control the dynamics of a sound.

Control surface A recording interface with dials and/or faders.

Cross-referencing Comparing sounds before and after adjustments, individually or in context.

Cue sheet Writing out a cue sheet *on a sheet of paper* as you work is invaluable for noting best takes, partial takes, edit points, where errors need to be repaired, or where changes in a mix happen. Using one saves a lot of time.

DAW Digital audio workstation.

Decibel (dB) Unit of measurement for sound.

Delay A repeat echo. Used judiciously, it can be a strong alternative to reverb, or be used in conjunction with it to minimise overlong reverb tails, or to add depth and presence.

Double tracking Recording a second, almost identical performance of a vocal or instrument; small differences in the two performances create a textural effect that can provide an attractive change of dynamic and tone, or help to shore up a less than perfect vocalist.

Dynamics The contrast in a mix, a performance, or musical arrangement; notably, changes in volume, rhythm, tone or mood.

Editing An essential tool to cut and paste waveforms, tighten up mix structures or performances, reduce or eliminate uncomfortable peaks, errors, extraneous noise, bulges, sibilance and plosives.

Engineer Person who understands the technical aspects of the recording studio they work in. They can be blamed if things go technically wrong.

Ensemble A group of musicians, vocalists or performers.

EQ (Equalisation) Basically, tone controls.

Extraneous noise Any unwanted ambient sound – computer noise, chatter, creaks, buzzes, or the neighbours complaining.

Fader A slider control on each channel of a mixing device.

Fidelity Literally, 'faith'; describing the sound quality of a recording (or lack of it).

Focal points Highlights in a mix such as vocals, instrumental solos, or changes of dynamics and tone.

Frequency The speed of the vibration of a sound wave. Higher frequencies have bigger values (kHz); lower frequencies smaller ones (Hz).

Gain structure The relative volume levels of all the components of the signal chain. It's important that all have strong levels without clipping or distortion.

Glyn Johns array Innovative technique for recording a drum kit with three microphones.

Interface A device with A/D converters that allows access to digital sound recording software. They range from a simple box with a microphone and line input, to complex mixing desks for recording and mixing multiple tracks.

'In the box' Recording and mixing with only a computer, without a mixing desk or ancillary equipment.

Latency A time lag on playback or recording in your DAW, due to insufficient RAM memory or incorrect audio drivers.

Level The volume (loudness) of a signal.

Limiter A compressor on stereo-oids.

Mastering The last stage of the recording process, to enhance a mix prior to release and distribution of the record. Ideally, it is to make the mix sound the same *but better*, or, all too often, compensate for the shortcomings of it.

Microphone placement The precise positioning of microphones.

Micing up The initial positioning of microphones.

Mixing The art of shaping and balancing multiple sounds into their final recorded form.

Mixing desk The art of shaping and balancing multiple sounds into their final recorded form with the aid of physical faders and knobs.

Monitoring Listening via loudspeakers or headphones.

Mono, 2-track, 4-track, 8-track, 16-track, 24-track Multitrack, analogue tape-recording formats; 32-track didn't really catch on.

Multiband compression A compressor that can be applied to multiple frequency bands and generally mess things up, especially if used over the stereo output of a mix.

Multitrack Recording on multiple, separate channels that can be manipulated later.

Musical arrangement A combination of instruments, each with structured parts or in a structured format.

Near-field monitors Small loudspeakers with one or two cones, designed for close range listening.

One more Do another take, if you please.

Outboard Ancillary hardware connected to a mixing desk or digital interface.

Overdub To record additional parts to an existing recording.

Panning The placement or movement of sound within a stereo field.

Parametric EQ Equalisation that can be applied to multiple frequencies selectively, in different amounts.

Passive listening Listening without preconceptions or focusing on any specific aspects of the recording; as if it were the first time you heard it.

Peak The maximum volume level a signal can reach without distortion.

Peak editing Manually reducing the loudest sounds of a recording.

Perceived volume The loudness a sound appears to have. This may differ from what the meters tell you.

Performance mixing The art of shaping and balancing multiple sounds into their final recorded form, manually and in real time, without the aid of automated technology, safety net or parachute.

Phase cancellation Holes in the sound made when frequencies compete and overlap, typically from poor microphone placement or the misuse of EQ.

Plosive A hard syllable, with an overly loud peak.

Plug-in A program that is plugged in digitally, as a supplement to the software bundled into a recording platform.

Portastudio Self-contained multitrack home-recording device, either analogue or digital, with limited capabilities.

Pre-production Preparation prior to a recording session.

Producer Person who tells everyone what to do in a recording session. They can be blamed if things go horribly wrong, or blame everyone else.

Punch-in Repair to an error on a selected part of a performance, either on a separate track, or the same one.

Record Most fondly, on 7in or 12in vinyl.

Reel to reel An analogue tape recorder using open reels of magnetic tape.

Relative level The volume/loudness of one sound in comparison to its companions.

Reverb Happens when sound travels from one end to the other of a space and bounces around in it. The bigger the space, the longer the reverb, plus the shape of the space will change the way it bounces.

Schedule List of works to be done and/or estimated time required to complete a recording session.

Sibilance Unwanted 'ess' or 'shh' sounds.

Song pyramid A way to help identify weaknesses and highlights in the structure of a song.

Sonics The 'sound' of a sound; its characteristics.

Sound on sound The only way to overdub prior to multitrack recording; dubs were recorded live when playing back the first track from one tape recorder and recording to a second machine whilst the dub was being performed. Once done, the recording could not be changed after the fact.

Submix A secondary mix, often made as an alternative, to repair an error, or insert as an edit into a remix.

Take Method of identifying a number of recorded performances, for example take one, take two, take three and so on.

Talkback Communication link from control room to studio via microphone or loudspeaker.

Tape compression An artefact of magnetic tape used in analogue reel to reel or cassette recorders that reduces peaks and troughs that occur in the signal in a natural and attractive way, commonly thought of as 'analogue sound'. Digital recording does the opposite, which is why you are reading this book.

Tape echo A superior analogue alternative to digital delay.

Three-way monitors Loudspeakers with three individual cones for treble, mid-range and bass.

Track An individual recording channel.

Track count The total number of individual sounds that comprise a completed recording.

Tracking Term describing the active 'recording' part of a recording session, as opposed to the preparatory or mixing aspects.

Transient A very fast, loud peak, often too quick for a compressor to catch.

Waveform Visual representation of a sound wave.

INDEX

TEMPLATE MIXING AND MASTERING

THE ULTIMATE GUIDE TO ACHIEVING A PROFESSIONAL SOUND

Featuring the full template used on sixteen No.1 songs!

BILLY DECKER AND **SIMON TAYLOR**

FOREWORD BY RODNEY ATKINS